CONTENTS

Introduction 5

One: Mythology Expressed by Joseph Campbell 9

Two: UFOs Perceived by George Adamski 27

Three: Scientology Organized by L. Ron Hubbard..........43

Four: Holistic Health Practiced by Norman Cousins 61

Five: The Psychic Life Celebrated by Shirley MacLaine 79

Six: The New Science Experienced by Fritjof Capra 97

Glossary 115

Resources 119

INTRODUCTION

One of my daughters recently gave me a T-shirt with a message inscribed on the back:
"Two things are sure in life: (1) There is a God, (2) You are not He."

This message alludes to three positions one can choose from regarding the existence of God. Two of these are familiar to everyone. Christians believe that God created the heavens and the earth and sustains us from moment to moment by his will. In contrast, the atheist says God does not exist, that only the material world is real. Christians have largely ignored the third position—a resurgence of an old idolatry—as they've concentrated on the threat of atheism.

In the last quarter of the twentieth century, however, the third position has made a dramatic comeback. While we have been concerned about one enemy, another somewhat more seductive one seems to have sneaked up on us in a "quiet revolution" spreading throughout North American culture. More and more adhere to the view that a human being and God are one and the same. Proponents claim we are leaving the so-called "Christian age" and rapidly moving toward a "higher," more "spiritual" level of existence. They assert that we are entering a *New Age* when people will cease to look to the Christian God for salvation and begin to realize that God is within them. Evil and suffering are illusions; raising our level of consciousness can solve humanity's problems. We need to be delivered from ignorance, they insist, not from evil. Self-love, they say, is more important than love for others or love for God. The whole New Age movement is captured in the figure of Shirley MacLaine standing on a California beach with arms outstretched, repeating over and over, "I am God."

New Age thought and practices are now spreading through many parts of our culture: sports, movies, music, business, education, psychology, and medicine. A 1992 survey revealed that large numbers of Americans follow New Age practices and concluded that "many who consider themselves good Christians nonetheless have engaged in practices that seemingly are counter to the teachings of their church." We have seen a rapid increase in meditation, the use of crystals to achieve power and healing, channeling of disembodied spirits, so-called "out-of-body" experiences, and attempts to divine the future and uncover past lives. Although some have argued that this is a passing fad, serious students of the movement all agree that we are witnessing a significant change in North American society.

When preparing to teach a college course on the New Age movement recently, I was surprised at how easy it was to find people eager to come and explain their New Age beliefs. Here's a sample of what they had to say:

- "Everything that is is God."
- "Jesus came to save me from my ignorance."
- "Guilt is a negative energy form."
- "Our purpose [in firewalking] is union with the natural world."
- "The earth is our mother."
- "Everything is an interactive organism."
- "We are inter-dimensional beings."
- "I channel Katumi."
- "Within our electromagnetic field we have seven energy centers called *Chakras.*"

Are these ideas far out and countercultural, or are they mainstreamed into our society? How can a neo-pagan, *monistic* view of the universe be spreading in the middle of a supposedly scientific, materialistic age? How have so many educated upper- and middle-class North Americans come to believe that ancient Hindu and Buddhist and Native American beliefs and practices are superior to both Christianity and materialism? Where do Christians draw the line?

In this book, I have tried to address these questions by studying the lives and beliefs of six prominent leaders in the New Age movement. Many others, of course, have also been influential, but these six are a sample of the variability within the movement and were chosen also because they simply are interesting people. By examining how each of these leaders came to be part of the movement and how others began to follow their lead, I hope to show what attracts people to the New Age and how such people think.

As Christians, we must understand what we are facing in the New Age movement if we are to counter the "wisdom" of the New Age with the wisdom of Christ. My T-shirt has another message on the front that gives the only proper response to the New Age:

"There is no other name under heaven given among mortals by which we must be saved" (Acts 4:12, NRSV).

Through your personal reflection and group discussion, I trust you will experience a deeper relationship with God and a renewed appreciation for a Reformed spirituality that will equip us to withstand the seductive power of the New Age movement.

—J. William Smit

ONE

MYTHOLOGY EXPRESSED BY JOSEPH CAMPBELL

Campbell's Journey to New Age
Joseph Campbell's New Age journey spanned almost his entire lifetime. An independent thinker, great storyteller, and teacher, Campbell openly opposed Christianity. Yet he has reaped popularity even among Christians, perhaps because of his tremendous influence on the Hollywood film industry. The popularity of *Star Wars*, which is based on Campbell's New Age views, confirms the seductive power of the New Age movement across our culture.

Early Influences
Campbell's interest in mythology began in 1910 when, at the age of six, he saw Buffalo Bill's Wild West show. Campbell later said, "I early became fascinated, seized, obsessed by the figure of a naked American Indian with his ear to the ground, a bow and arrow in his hand, and a look of special knowledge in his eyes" (Stephen and Robin Larsen, *A Fire in the Mind*). The idea that such a person might have "special knowledge" marked Joseph Campbell's life and, partly because of his influence, still infuses the New Age movement today.
Joseph attended school in New Rochelle, New York, until his mother enrolled him at a Catholic boarding school in Connecticut. He excelled in academics, athletics, music, and drama, and wrote essays for his school's literary journal. In 1921, as a freshman at Dartmouth College, Campbell wrote, "Complete disorientation, religious doubts

beginning. . . ." His "disorientation" included questioning Catholic doctrine as a result of exposure to evolutionary theory in biology.

Joseph transferred to Columbia University. Still fascinated with Native North Americans, he also took courses with the famous anthropologist, Franz Boas, at Barnard College. Sir James Frazer's famous work, *The Golden Bough*, introduced him to ancient myths about the renewal of the earth through the death of a king and became "the second of [his] long series of bibles." He saw a parallel with Jesus Christ, but at this point he still considered one myth and the other religion.

Traveling by ship to Europe with his family for sightseeing and the 1924 Olympic games, Campbell met and established a friendship with Jiddu Krishnamurti, a young Indian mystic. Krishnamurti obviously influenced Campbell, probably most significantly in his teaching that one should concentrate on self-knowledge and reject the spiritual authority of anyone else. On this trip, Campbell also became acquainted with the ideas of Sigmund Freud through *Totem and Tabu*, which he purchased in a Paris bookstore.

After graduating from Columbia, uncertain what to do next, he eventually joined his father's hosiery business. He disrupted the workplace with his systematic questioning of other employees about their feelings regarding work and life in general. Realizing that he would not be happy in the business world, he looked elsewhere for what he later would call his *bliss*.

"Maverick Scholar"

Campbell's search led him to people who were fascinated by psychology and mysticism. He returned to Columbia as a graduate student, and his impressive master's thesis research in mythology secured him a fellowship at the University of Paris to continue his medieval studies in the fall of 1927.

In Paris he stopped a man carrying a book that looked interesting to him and thus met Herbert King Stone. This American professor became his mentor and granted him access to his extensive library of medieval literature. Stone wrote to a friend, "Joseph Campbell is the most perfect embodiment of everything beautiful, fine and lovable in Youth that I have ever known. . . . He knows about many cults and 'isims' and rejects them all. . . . May the God he is seeking bless him forever and forever. There will never be another Joe."

With his fellowship extended a year, he went to Germany in the fall of 1928. He later wrote that the great German scholars, such as Goethe, showed him the "mythic dimension" of what he was studying.

Their teachings paralleled what he was learning from his friend Krishnamurti.

After a few months in Germany, he launched his long study of the works of Sigmund Freud and Carl Jung. Both Freud and Jung believed that ancient mythology could be useful in understanding the workings of the human mind, but it was Campbell who propelled this idea forward in extensive analysis of mythology.

Campbell, more interested in Jung than in Freud, eventually (in 1971) published *The Portable Jung,* considered a "masterpiece of condensation" of Jung's extensive writings. In trying to explain his occult experiences, Jung developed two ideas that strongly influenced Campbell's later work and are now an integral part of New Age thought. The first: *archetypes,* defined as "universal primordial images passed down from an ancestral past that includes not only early humankind but humankind's prehuman and animal ancestors." Archetypes, Jung said, though subconscious, influence behavior and have always formed the basis of thought.

Campbell also adopted Jung's idea of the *collective unconscious,* the storehouse of the shared archetypal memories that most, if not all, people carry. The collective unconscious, according to Jung, exists at a deeper level than individual unconscious, which Freud said develops in childhood. Previous generations pass down the collective unconscious, which is present at birth. Thus Jung introduced a new way to interpret the experiences of spiritualists and others who claim contact with supernatural forces: they are particularly open to the collective unconscious.

During his year in Germany, Campbell deserted his Catholicism and stopped going to church. He aimed for freedom from "the constraints placed upon you by the opinions of your friends and your society." "It is," he wrote, "through experience that the soul grows. . . . Through the elimination thus of desires, desire for security, for approval, for might, one reduces oneself to the single great desire for union with God." Rejecting the authority of the church and the Bible, he depended on personal experience to teach him what is true and real. In fact, he embraced total relativism, claiming, "There is no truth, only experience." Ironically, this one who perceived himself as so independent did not recognize his new friends' obvious influence in bringing him to this monistic view of "union with God." (*Monism,* the belief that all that exists is one continuous reality, lies at the heart of the New Age movement. This basic theme characterizes the beliefs of the six leaders we will study.)

Campbell returned to the United States in 1929. With his family in financial straits, he sought a way to make a living. In his journal he wrote, "I think I'll probably use my whole life up attempting to decide in which direction I ought to go." He also summarized his religious position: "I believe in an ultimate question mark; in the importance to myself of my own sensations; and in Self Perfection as the most likely justification for any existence."

"The maverick scholar," as Campbell later called himself, explained that at this time "the whole range of my studies became now coordinated under the sign of an as yet only dimly foreseen meaning of the magic word: Mythos," a word often repeated in the works of Jung. *Myth* to him did not mean a story with no basis in truth, told only for entertainment. Rather, *myth* could "open the mind and heart to the utter wonder of all being."

"Mythology," he said, "is metaphor. God, angels, purgatory, these are metaphors." He believed that metaphor and symbolic images are the only way to talk of something ultimately inexpressible. Throughout history, myths have expressed our powerful feelings about what life means to us. Although they have also been used to support both religion and social structures, he thought the most important use today is psychological, helping people in their self-understanding and self-development. "The imagery of mythology is symbolic of spiritual powers within us." Myth, he believed, is what people use to understand their own experiences in the context of other people's experiences. He argued that a collapse of true myth is partly to blame for the rise in crime, suicide, addictions, broken homes, and delinquency.

Career Paths

Campbell eventually accepted a teaching position at Sarah Lawrence, a recently established women's college, where he stayed for thirty-eight years. He wrote to a friend that he wanted to show his students "the well of mythology that lies beneath [the Middle Ages]" and "the connection of that mythology with the deepest places in themselves." His combination of erudition, enthusiasm, and good looks popularized him among Sarah Lawrence students. After a few years he cut back to a three-quarter teaching load to allow himself more time for his research and writing.

In 1943, Campbell's first book was published in collaboration with Maud Oakes, a young artist. *Where the Two Came to Their Father* described Navajo sand painting. Followers of Jung enjoyed its Jungian archetypes. In 1944, he wrote a commentary for a new edition of *Grimm's Fairy Tales*. The difference between a fairy tale and a myth, he claimed, is that although the fairy tale is meant to entertain and is not to be taken as seriously as a myth, it can also instruct.

Campbell had been introduced to James Joyce's mythological themes in *Ulysses*, so when Joyce's *Finnegan's Wake* was published, Campbell read it eagerly. He and Henry Morton Robinson, who later became famous as the author of *The Cardinal*, spent many days together trying to interpret its meanings. Their results were published in 1944 as *A Skeleton Key to Finnegan's Wake* and received highly favorable reviews.

By the age of forty, Joseph Campbell was becoming a well-known figure, and his popularity opened up new opportunities. In 1949, after many rejections and revisions, his first widely read and still best-known work, *The Hero with a Thousand Faces*, was published. It introduced the idea that an archetype—called *"monomyth"* by Campbell —of the hero is found in many societies around the world throughout history, thus giving a thousand faces to one figure.

Hero's immediate popularity remains; it reached the best-seller list as recently as 1989. In the sixties, it was very popular on college campuses, along with Heinlein's *Stranger in a Strange Land* and Tolkien's *The Lord of the Rings*. (Supposedly many young people thought these books offered "a way out of the trap of the secular.") *Hero* contains many interesting stories and what one reviewer called "the mystical and pseudo-philosophic fog of Jung." Campbell's theory that myths arise from the collective unconscious was controversial. He also treated the story of Jesus Christ as merely one of many myths, fitting a common pattern and therefore not unique.

Having already written much about the Orient, Campbell finally went to see it for himself in 1954. He was surprised that people in India wanted to talk about politics and patriotism and was shocked by the communist leanings of many educated Indians. Instead of utopia, he encountered dramatic extremes of poverty and wealth, disease, and inferior treatment of women. He had condemned Christian missionaries going to places such as India, but now he admitted, "Christian benefits cannot be shrugged away."

He preferred Japan to India—cleaner, more efficient, better educated, and not anti-American. Japan, he believed, was adjusting to modern society with an attitude of "progressive spirituality." When a Japanese professor inquired about his religion, Campbell said, "Since I found that all the great religions were saying essentially the same thing in various ways, I was unable and unwilling to commit myself to any one." He initiated an intensive study of the Japanese language, religion, and mythology, and now claimed a new and broader perspective from which to view religion and mythology.

Returning to his teaching at Sarah Lawrence, Campbell frequently spoke at conferences in the United States and Europe. In 1966, he gave his first annual lecture at the Esalen Institute, probably the best known and most influential center for New Age thinking. He also delivered periodic lectures to State Department foreign service officers facing new assignments. Most significantly, however, he began work on a multi-volume publication, *The Masks of God,* which was to become his "mid-life magnum opus." "Every deity," he said, "is a metaphor, a mask, for the ultimate mystery ground, the transcendent energy source of the universe, that is also the mysterious source of your own life and everyone else's."

Published over a period of years, the four volumes of *The Masks of God* are entitled *Primitive Mythology, Oriental Mythology, Occidental Mythology,* and *Creative Mythology.* He strove to break through the ethnocentric limitations of even the most educated Americans and show them, through an overview of world mythology, the universal dimensions of human experience. He wrote that "themes such as the fire, theft, deluge, land of the dead, virgin birth, and resurrected hero have a worldwide distribution—appearing everywhere in new combinations while remaining, like the elements of a kaleidoscope, only a few and always the same." He believed that these common, ancient stories contain the meaning of religion and myth.

A New Age Leader

Heinrich Zimmer, a German student of mythology, taught Campbell to look for truth in what we most love. Zimmer called this one's *delight*; Campbell named it one's *bliss*—"follow your bliss" became his most quoted expression. This meant a careful self-study to determine the most helpful road in becoming more fully alive.

Campbell's hero archetype is a person who "ventures forth from the world of common day into a region of supernatural wonder." For Campbell, the hero's journey reflects the personal development of the individual. Native American, Oriental, European medieval, and Christian traditions all tell of the "discovery of the self." This self is the inner person, which is eternal and part of a universal consciousness. Hero stories about heroes are means to express something important to each of us, the personal journey each of us should take toward enlightenment.

Although the myth tells a story of adventure, Campbell argued that it is actually about a person's psychological encounter with god and goddess figures such as the Virgin Mary. We must all integrate the two sides of our nature, male and female, to achieve enlightenment. We also need to balance what we see as good and evil within us. Campbell said that "by overcoming dark passions, the hero symbolizes our ability to control the irrational savage within us."

The hero, then, is the self, with great creative powers that one can choose to release. "The essence of oneself and the essence of the world: these two are one." The decision to follow one's bliss begins a hero's journey; the heroic journey ends with the discovery of the collective unconscious and achieving a state of bliss.

The journey to bliss has become an accepted part of New Age thinking. Many New Agers, however, overlook Campbell's teaching that bliss comes only with sacrifice and hard work. They cling to the sixties' counterculture call to "do your own thing." The lack of moral direction in this injunction does not trouble them. What if your greatest bliss harms others? New Agers seem to think that each person following his or her personal bliss, without conscious direction, will work out for the good of all. This wishful thinking exposes Campbell's inconsistency. He favors law and order and dislikes hippies and other free-wheeling types, but his writings divulge distrust of social norms and advise looking within rather than to others for direction.

His frequent use of the word *synchronicity* further indicates his influence in the New Age movement; likely Campbell is responsible for integrating this Jungian term into New Age jargon. To Jung, it means a connection between two things without any apparent cause—what we might call a "meaningful coincidence." Campbell uses the word to explain many events of his own life as well as many historic incidents. Rather than choosing from chance, determinism, and individual choice—not to mention predestination—Campbell opts for a mystical interplay of forces in the universe, of which individual choice is one. *Synchronicity* meant to Campbell that although we cannot control our lives nor prevent all pain and tragedy, we can take advantage of seeming coincidences to experience life more fully. He believed in an "All" of which everyone is a part, yet he warned against becoming too absorbed in that "All." Individual experience, individual bliss, is ultimately most important to him. This adjustment of Eastern monism to fit Western individualism exemplifies the New Age movement's eclectic beliefs.

Ironically, Campbell's fame grew immensely through the influence of television and films, two media he had criticized and largely ignored. Campbell was "transformed from teacher and scholar . . . into a bona fide media sensation," or, more critically, "from a harmless eccentric into a dangerous mischief-maker."

Campbell was introduced to television audiences in the biography *The Hero's Journey,* and then in *The Transformation of Myth Through Time,* a series developed from his last lecture tour. His greatest exposure by far, however, came from *The Power of Myth,* a six-hour series with journalist Bill Moyers, first shown on PBS in 1988 shortly after his death. Thousands of copies of these tapes have been sold for personal and college classroom showing. Much of the material soon appeared in a best-selling book of the same title. Moyers himself explained the interviews' popularity:

> *Someone said of Joe that he was the best teacher you ever had, the best grandfather you ever had, the best uncle, who told you stories—there was something of that. Then there was the crisp simple power of his persona, especially his eyes, his face as he talked . . . he was a natural. It was intimate television. . . . There was the power of his stories and how they connected to life. . . . It was not really a series about mythology but about living . . . (It) was something like . . . giving us the vocabulary for a new effort to define what it means to be spiritual today. The old stories don't work anymore. . . . The traditional biblical construct which for centuries helped people find their place, raise their children, define their roles, answer their questions—that's been dying away, as you know, for a long time. And here was a man on television talking about old stories that could be looked at in new ways, stories that helped people discover again what it means to be spiritual.*

Said one commentator, "Campbell's students, readers, and audiences took him at his word and went back to the original sources in droves, helping revitalize the moribund interest in mythology and, more, breathed new life into them, translated the stories and images into our art, sculpture, theater, film, poetry, science, religious studies. His vast influence on pop culture and catalyzing of cross-cultural discussions over matters of the spiritual validates his maverick scholarship."

Although most people don't recognize it, nowhere has Campbell's influence been stronger than in the Hollywood film industry. "No book has come close to influencing contemporary movies as pervasively as . . . *The Hero with a Thousand Faces.*" *Hero* has become "a bible for modern filmmakers" because it outlines a successful adventure story. Not all films remain true to Campbell's ideas, of course, but he has introduced many New Ages concepts, most significantly monism and spiritualism. *Myth* is now a popular word in the entertainment industry, even on the level of comic books and children's stories.

Near the end of his life, Campbell finally accepted an invitation from George Lucas to watch the *Star Wars* trilogy at his Skywalker Ranch. Lucas himself is represented in these films by the hero figure, Luke Skywalker, while Yoda, the wise sage, represents Campbell.

Lucas says that the *Star Wars* films as well as his *Indiana Jones* series, both among the most popular films of all time, are based on Campbell's ideas. When Moyers asked him if *Star Wars* gives us a good model of a hero, Campbell replied, "It's good, sound teaching, I would say."

The success of *Star Wars* marked a "return to enchantment"—a new interest in ancient myths. Hollywood still calls us away from normal routine into an adventure; the recent film *The Lion King,* for example, was highly popular.

Although some say in his defense that Campbell was "not just a New Age prophet," his academic colleagues paid him little mind, and his most loyal followers today are in the New Age movement. All his life he advised people to rise above the ethnocentrism of their own culture, yet in the end Campbell expresses common American values: "individualism, democracy, romantic love, admiration for the selfless hero, disdain for intellectualism, emphasis on experiencing life." Although he constantly attacked the church, Campbell has also become popular among many church-going people.

In his last years, Campbell was hailed as a hero, a sage, a popularizer of mythology, and a synthesizer of Eastern and Western religion. After his death, he was accused of racism, anti-Semitism, and anti-feminism. "Follow your bliss" was accused of contributing to "selfishness on a colossal scale," and Campbell has been labeled a priest of the new religion of self-development. All these charges are hotly debated. Regardless of how much truth they contain, they pale in importance compared to the influence of his central and clearly anti-Christian teaching of monism. Unfortunately, even Christians express little concern about this.

What Is *Mythology?*

Lies or Truth?

Two weeks before his conversion, C. S. Lewis went for an evening walk with J. R. R. Tolkien. Lewis told Tolkien that he understood the power of myth to "awe, delight, and inspire," but ultimately "myths were lies and therefore worthless, even though breathed through silver." Tolkien disagreed. He argued that since God made us in his image, he must have given us our imagination, so the myths we create can contain God-given truths. This argument convinced Lewis. Both of them proceeded to create entertaining and instructive Christian myths.

Lewis and Tolkien distinguished between Christian and pagan myths but believed that pagan myths sometimes hold truth. In *Mere Christianity,* Lewis wrote, "God sent the human race what I call good dreams: I mean those queer stories scattered all through the heathen religions about a god who dies and comes to life again, and by his death, has somehow given new life to men." Elsewhere he says that since we all share the "divine light" we should "expect to find in the imagination of great pagan teachers and myth-makers some glimpse of that theme which we believe to be the very plot of the whole cosmic story—the theme of incarnation, death and rebirth."

Lewis and Tolkien also differentiate between myths that recount historical fact and fiction that, like their own stories, convey truth. Pagan stories of death and rebirth are all set in some indeterminate time and place. In contrast, Lewis says, the Christian story is about "a historical personage, whose execution can be dated pretty accurately, under a named Roman magistrate. It is not the difference between falsehood and truth. It is the difference between a real event on the one hand and dim dreams or premonitions of that same event on the other." And again, "The heart of Christianity is a myth which is also a fact."

Tolkien and Lewis would agree with Campbell that myths are important but would disagree that ultimately all myths teach monism. On the contrary, if many myths contain a common theme (what Campbell calls a *monomyth*), it is that humanity has fallen and needs a Savior who will restore the earth.

Spiritual, Not Religious?

New Agers typically think of themselves as spiritual but not religious; according to Moyers, Campbell helped people understand the difference. Religion implies organization, creeds, rituals, discipline, membership—everything typically necessary in a church. New Agers, usually individualistic, resist such structures and controls. They want to be spiritual and look within themselves to discover their true relationship to the universe. Campbell told them that mythology can help them, but religion hinders this project. Religion ("misunderstood mythology") errs by taking literally that which was meant to be metaphor; it "turns poetry into prose." Campbell accepts none of the Bible stories as historical truth. He blamed religion for the fact that many people take them literally and quoted Jung to the effect that religion can hinder the experience of god.

The New Age opinion that people can get along just fine without religion seems naive, considering humanity's history. In all times and places, in every society, people have organized religions. Sociologists agree that humanity has a functional need for religion; we cannot get along without such structures. Although a few go their own way, people in general, by organizing religious systems, have maintained beliefs and practices having to do with God and what they consider ultimately important. Many New Agers are already part of religious organizations such as Scientology, the Institute of Noetic Sciences, the Church Universal and Triumphant, Esalen Institute, Self-Realization Fellowship, and Synchronicity Foundation. History predicts that if the New Age movement is to have a lasting influence, it will continue to move toward greater structure, effectively becoming a religion—probably with many denominations and splinter groups, but nevertheless an identifiable religion. That process seems already well underway.

The New Age Jesus

The New Age view of Jesus is thoroughly and competently reviewed in *Revealing the New Age Jesus* by Douglas Groothuis. He says that most New Agers, although lacking unanimity, would agree to several ideas:

- Jesus is revered or respected as a highly spiritually evolved being who serves as an example for further evolution.

- The individual, personal, historical Jesus is separated from the universal, impersonal, eternal Christ or Christ Consciousness. . . . Jesus is regarded as *a* Christ.

- The orthodox understanding of Jesus as the supreme and final revelation of God is dismissed as illegitimate . . . [because it] limits the power of God.

- Jesus' death on the cross (if recognized at all) is not accepted as having any ethical significance for salvation.

- Jesus' resurrection from the dead is not viewed as a physical fact [but rather] a spiritual triumph not unique to Jesus.

- Jesus' "second coming" is not a literal, physical, and visible return [but] a stage in the evolutionary advancement of the race when the Christic energies escape the confinements of ignorance.

- Exotic, extra-biblical documents are regarded as sources for authentic material about the life of Jesus not available from the canonical Scriptures.

To support these contentions, New Agers refer to a variety of ancient sources. Most commonly they appeal to the Gnostic writings discovered in Nag Hammadi, Egypt, in 1945. Another source, which they profess to be an ancient Tibetan document, says that between the ages of thirteen and twenty-nine, Jesus studied in the Far East. People like Shirley MacLaine claim that Jesus belonged to the Essene Brotherhood, even though the New Testament never mentions this group. (Groothuis shows that the Dead Sea Scrolls and other materials demonstrate the Essenes' beliefs were not New Age; the argument that they were is based on false or nonexistent documents.) New Agers claim that *A Course in Miracles* and some other recent writings are channeled directly from Jesus. These writings consistently teach an unbiblical, New Age view of Jesus, including many of the points summarized above.

Christians may be shocked that Campbell can find stories from other times and places that correspond to parts of the story of Jesus. This need not lead to the conclusion, however, that the correlation lies in the existence of a mystical unity and that nothing in the Bible is to be taken literally. As Tolkien and Lewis suggest, stories of every culture express the basic reality of sin and the need for salvation.

Parallel to Gnosticism?

Gnosticism has been defined as a "dualistic, mystical Christian religion, which flourished in the Mediterranean region during the second century A.D. Gnostics believed that redemption, or liberation of the soul, was possible only through knowledge *(gnosis)*, not faith." Although today people commonly speak of Gnosticism as a form of Christianity, the early church quickly rejected it as heretical. Gnosticism was not a unified, coherent phenomenon; it covered a wide variety of sects at various times and places. Gnostics drew on ideas from a great variety of sources: Greek, Babylonian, Iranian, Egyptian, Jewish, and Christian. They had in common a desire for knowledge that was not so much intellectual as intuitive and mystical, springing from "the spark of divinity" they believed was within them. Knowledge of God, they thought, came only through knowledge of self, which they considered a part of God. Their goal was the release of the inner self from what they considered the bondage of this world.

Gnosticism differs from orthodox Christianity on many important points:

- Gnosticism is elitist. It divides humanity into the knowers (Gnostics) and the ignorant, and teaches that only the knowers will be saved. Christianity teaches that all with faith in Christ will be saved—not from ignorance, but from sin.

- The central myth of Gnosticism is that the universe is the bungled creation of a secondary god who falsely claims superiority to the true high God. Humans, spiritual parts of the high God, find themselves trapped in this imperfect physical world. Christians believe in one God, who created a good but now fallen earth. Humans are part of his creation, made in his image, but not part of him.

- Jesus, to the Gnostics, was a great teacher sent by the high God to bring *gnosis*, but not part of the Trinity. Perceiving the material world as evil, inferior, or illusion, Gnostics could not accept the incarnation of God in human form. Like many in the New Age today, Gnostics separated Jesus from the Christ, a heresy against which early Christian theologians fought diligently. Christians know only one Christ; Gnostics recognize many.

Gnosticism is reviving partly because of the influence of "neo-Gnostics" like Carl Jung, who claimed that "Christianity and Western culture have suffered grievously because of the repression of the Gnostic approach to religion." But is gnosticism a significant part of the New Age movement? In his recent prize-winning and best-selling book *The Gnostic Empire Strikes Back*, Peter Jones says, "Recently I have discovered that New Age religion and Gnosticism . . . resemble one another like two Siamese cats," and points out many parallels. Clearly, Gnostic beliefs have strongly influenced the New Age. Campbell, for example, refers often to Gnostic texts.

Several differences lie between Gnosticism and the New Age, however. Most significantly, the Gnostics were dualistic, trying to separate good spirit from evil matter; New Agers are monistic, arguing that the physical universe is good and one with God. Interested in things spiritual, they in no way reject the world and often exhibit great concern about nature and ecology. Secondly, the ancient Gnostics generally treated women as inferior to men. The Gnostic *Gospel of Thomas* quotes Jesus saying, "For every woman who will make herself male will enter the kingdom of heaven"—hardly a teaching to cheer the heart of a New Ager. Thirdly, Groothuis points out that New Agers often give modern, psychological interpretation to Gnostic texts and ignore whatever they find distasteful, such as the hierarchy of spiritual beings. So, although Gnosticism strongly influences the New Age, to claim that New Age mythology is but a revival of Gnosticism is oversimplification.

Mythology and the Christian

Following his visits to India and Japan, Campbell wrote in his journal, "Clearly Christianity is opposed fundamentally and intrinsically to everything that I am working and living for; and for the modern world, I believe, with all of its faiths and traditions, Krishna is a *much* better teacher and model than Christ." He failed to notice this statement is inconsistent with his belief that all religions teach the same thing. New Agers accept "many paths to the one God," of which Christianity is an acceptable alternative. On the other hand, they explicitly reject Christianity, a rejection that seems inevitable if a person truly understands its claim that Christ is the only path to God.

Campbell understood the basis for this rejection of Christianity, and in a later work he clarifies that this is precisely his objection:

> *The difficulty faced today by Christian thinkers . . . follows from their doctrine of the Nazarene as the* unique *historical incarnation of God; and in Judaism, likewise, there is the no less troublesome doctrine of a universal God whose eye is on but one Chosen People of all in his created world. The fruit of such ethnocentric historicism is poor spiritual fare today; and the increasing difficulties of our clergies in attracting gourmets to their banquets should be evidence enough that there must be something no longer palatable about the dishes they are serving.*

The hope of the future to Campbell lies not in the church, not in the government, not, indeed, in any organization at all, but in "the free association of men and women of like spirit . . . not a handful but a thousand heroes, ten thousand heroes, who will create a future image of what humankind can be."

Campbell leaves us with a sort of elitism. To him, the hero is what everyone should be but only a few ever achieve. He asserts that only "the best part of man" concern themselves with trying to create their own mythology and fully experience life. Those unwilling to create their own mythology he describes as "the supine that must have their life values given them, cried at them from the pulpits and other mass media of the day." By contrast, he believed in "a great deal of deep spiritual quest and finding now in progress in this world, outside the sanctified social centers, beyond their purview and control, in small groups, here and there, and more often . . . by ones and twos" (seemingly the creative artists and writers who formed his circle of friends).

Campbell advocated individual freedom, but as Eric Hoffer once said, "When people are free to do as they please, they usually imitate each other." Campbell, in his contempt for those who learn their values from the pulpit, demonstrates a severe weakness in his view of the relationship between the individual and society. He seems blind to the extent to which our social context shapes us and how utterly lost we would be without it. He says that the church has now lost control and "each individual is the center of a mythology of his own." This is an obvious overstatement. Perhaps we are more free than previous generations to create our own beliefs, but the choices are certainly limited, and all of us, including Campbell, are incapable of finding our way without direction from others.

Campbell's blatant rejection of Christianity leaves little doubt as to the incompatibility of his New Age views with Paul's words in Galations 5:1: "It is for freedom that Christ has set us free. Stand firm, then. . . ." Jesus' words to the Jews who had once believed in him add a qualifier: *"If you hold to my teaching,* you are really my disciples. Then you will know the truth, and the truth will set you free" (John 8:31-32).

Suggestions for Group Session

Getting Started

Begin this first session by introducing yourselves. You may want to share what sparked your interest in the topic of New Age. These suggestions for your group session will assume that you have read the chapter in advance.

Merriam-Webster's Collegiate Dictionary, Tenth Edition defines mythology as "an allegorical narrative; a body of myths: as the myths dealing with the gods, demigods, and legendary heroes of a particular people." Joseph Campbell would agree that myths are symbolic images, but he believes they are much more than stories. "The imagery of mythology is symbolic of spiritual powers within us," he states, and myths are what people use to understand themselves and their own experiences.

We probably agree with J. R. R. Tolkien that imagination is from God. He created us with the ability to dream and pretend, evidenced already in young children. But unless this imagination is God-driven and God-serving, we must concede with C. S. Lewis that the power of myth to "awe, delight, and inspire" is "worthless, even though breathed through silver." After his conversion, Lewis creatively and powerfully used myth to convey God-given truths in his literary works. Oh, that Campbell had been so driven!

Campbell's early interest in mythology and continual search for "bliss" ultimately led him to reject Christianity and the Christ of Scripture. His New Age ideas, especially monism (the belief that all is one) and individual spirituality (his "hero's search for bliss"), have found their way into popular culture, especially influencing Hollywood's film industry. Many of us may have encountered Campbell's New Age mythology there—unawares.

The following discussion questions and activities are designed to help your group develop an increased awareness of the negative influences of mythology with its New Age message on our culture. While Joseph Campbell's *Hero* has become a Hollywood "bible," *God's* Bible is still the word of truth for Christians everywhere.

Begin this session with a prayer to thank God for giving us creative minds and the gift of imagination and to ask him to guard our hearts and minds from that which is not true.

Group Discussion and Activity

1. Read 1 Timothy 1:3-7 and Titus 1:10-16. In these two passages, Paul warns his spiritual sons, Timothy and Titus, about heretical teachers in the church. In the *NIV Study Bible* notes for the passage from 1 Timothy, these teachers are characterized by these practices:

- teaching false doctrines;
- teaching Jewish myths;
- wanting to be teachers of the Old Testament law;
- building up endless, far-fetched, fictitious stories based on obscure genealogical points;
- conceit;
- being argumentative;
- meaningless and foolish talk;
- not knowing what they were talking about;
- teaching ascetic practices;
- and using their positions of religious leadership for personal financial gain.

Do any of these characteristics describe Joseph Campbell? What evidence from this chapter supports your answer?

2. If you agree that some of the characteristics Paul used to describe heretical teachers of his day also apply to Campbell, what warning would you give your spiritual sons and daughters about him?

3. Campbell was influenced by Krishnamurti, an Indian mystic, whom he said "set me off on a quest for something which I scarcely understand." Philip Yancey, author of *The Jesus I Never Knew,* is also on a quest. Yancey asks himself if his childhood impressions of Jesus had been confirmed and wonders what he as an adult truly thinks about this Jesus. How does this search for a deeper understanding of the Christ we met in church and church school differ from the search for a god who wears masks in mystic stories?

4. Although at one point Campbell had scorned the idea of Christian missionaries going to places like India, after his visit to India he said, "Christian benefits cannot be shrugged away." Aside from the obvious spiritual benefits, what other benefits does Christian influence often bring to a culture? (Consider health and literacy programs, agricultural and cottage industry training, and similar acts of mercy brought to foreign fields by missionaries who came primarily to spread the gospel.) Is a servant attitude present in Campbell's "hero"?

5. Is the message about God's only begotten Son "poor spiritual fare today," as Campbell says? Should pastors be concerned about the "increasing difficulties . . . in attracting gourmets to their banquets . . . " and "realize that there must be something no longer palatable about the dishes they are serving"?

6. Read Matthew 22:1-14. The *NIV Matthew Henry Commentary* says *"Oxen and fattened cattle are butchered* for the feast; no delicacies, but substantial food; enough, and enough of the best. . . . The guests *are invited. . . .* None are excluded but those who exclude themselves." How does this perspective influence what pastors and churches serve to attract the hungry as opposed to the "gourmets"?

7. How would you explain "meaningful coincidence," what Campbell called *synchronicity,* from a biblical Reformed perspective? What evidence can you give from your own life that "all things, in fact, come to us not by chance but from his fatherly hand" (Heidelberg Catechism, A 27).

8. Does the New Age influence on the film-making industry surprise you? How can we discern this influence? As Christian consumers, how do we respond to it?

9. Read 1 Corinthians 1:18-25. Did C. S. Lewis accurately explain the foolishness of the cross when he said, "The heart of Christianity is a myth which is also a fact"? How can we accept this "myth"?

Closing

Read together the words of this contemporary testimony:

Being both God and man,
Jesus is the only Mediator
between God and his people.
He alone paid the debt of our sin;
there is no other Savior!
In him the Father chose those

whom he would save.
His electing love sustains our hope:
God's grace is free
to save sinners who offer nothing
but their need for mercy.

Our new life in Christ
is celebrated and nourished
in the fellowship of congregations
where God's name is praised,
his Word proclaimed,
his way taught;
where sins are confessed,
prayers and gifts are offered,
and sacraments are celebrated.

—*Our World Belongs to God,* 28, 39

Close this session with a prayer of thanksgiving that through his Spirit, God works faith in us to accept the gospel message of God's grace.

TWO

UFOS PERCEIVED BY GEORGE ADAMSKI

Adamski's Journey to New Age

In the early forties, long before space walks and visits to the moon, George Adamski was fascinated with UFOs. Although we might attribute flying saucers and strangers from outer space to vivid imaginations, Adamski's "space brothers" theology, firmly rooted in *monism*, has become a powerful anti-Christian religious movement.

Early Influences

Born in Poland in 1891, George Adamski immigrated to New York with his parents when he was one year old. He acquired from his Catholic parents "an unusual and deeply religious approach to the wonders of creation." Adamski, who had little formal education, later claimed that he learned from the "university of the world" and "grew into adulthood with wonder and reverence toward all phases of nature."

For fifteen years (called the "lost years" by his followers) following his six-year Army assignment, Adamski reportedly "traveled around the nation, earning his living at any job that offered," searching for knowledge and wisdom, and lecturing on philosophy in the Southwest. During this period he became a member of the Ancient and Mystical Order Rosae Crucis. AMORC, founded in 1909, is an American branch of the Rosicrucians, a group that claims to date back to the ancient Egyptians. Most scholars believe it actually originated with Christian Rosenkreutz, a fourteenth-century German teacher of occult practices. AMORC members believe that they can rise through levels of "cosmic consciousness" until, after several reincarnations, they may be admitted to the highest level, the Illuminati, and "direct communication with a higher source." The greatest goal of the Rosicrucian is to "achieve a greater oneness with the Supreme Being."

Career Paths

In his forties, Adamski finally settled down in Laguna Beach, California, established a "monastery," and began to teach "the universal laws" and "mastery of life" to hundreds of students. He called himself the "Founder of Universal Progressive Christianity, Royal Order of Tibet."

In 1936 Adamski published a small book with the cover title *Wisdom of the Masters of the Far East*. The inside title page reads "Questions and Answers by the Royal Order of Tibet, Vol. 1, Compiled by Professor G. Adamski." Monism is the major teaching in this book, which starts with, "In the beginning was Consciousness, and Consciousness was with God, and Consciousness is God." God, he said, is both the Cause or Father of all creation and the creation itself. The Universe *is* God; "God is everywhere because he is the Totality." Although the elaboration on this theme and his stories of personal experiences grew more fantastic and incredible over the years, he never abandoned this monistic religious core.

In 1940, Adamski and a few of his disciples moved from Laguna Beach to a ranch near Mount Palomar. Adamski took advantage of the area's ideal conditions for observing the night sky and became an amateur astronomer. He later claimed that soon after moving to Mount Palomar, he began to see strange objects in the night sky.

During a meteor shower on October 9, 1946, he and some of his friends were amazed at a large, black, cigar-shaped object in the sky. It lingered quite close to them in one spot before it "pointed its nose upward and quickly shot up into space, leaving a fiery trail behind it." This experience first led Adamski to consider the possibility of interplanetary travel. Adamski became obsessed with unidentified flying objects (UFOs).

Along with attempting to capture these strange objects on film, Adamski decided to try his hand at science fiction. In 1949, he published *Pioneers of Space: A Trip to the Moon, Mars and Venus*, actually ghostwritten by a follower, Lucy McGinnis. Not many copies were printed; it is now a rare book. In the forward, Adamski thought it unlikely that God would create such a vast universe and populate only a small corner of it. He believed in many inhabited planets and that, "given the law of progress," some of them must be much more advanced than ours.

By the early fifties, Adamski had gained celebrity status, appealing particularly to those who believed in a government cover-up of UFOs. After many inclusive photos of "something . . . moving out there," in 1951 he produced and published what many considered an amazing series of four photos. The first one shows a large, cigar-shaped object with a smaller saucer-shaped glow above it. More saucer-shaped lights appear in the next photos. Adamski claimed that they showed a large "mother ship" releasing small "scout ships." Adamski sold copies of these photos through the mail, thus becoming acquainted with many people around the world who were interested in flying saucers.

In November of 1952, Adamski began what has been called the "extraterrestrial contact movement." After hearing rumors of flying saucers landing in the desert not far from his home, he and two couples from Arizona plus Alice Wells, manager of the small restaurant on his property, and Lucy McGinnis set out to find these objects. Following Adamski's hunches (or, according to others, directions Wells received in a trance), they were looking around when, "suddenly . . . riding high, and without sound, there was a gigantic cigar-shaped silvery ship, without wings or appendages of any kind. Slowly, almost as if it was drifting, it came in our direction; then seemed to stop, hovering motionless."

In about five minutes a small saucer-type UFO appeared and settled to the ground and a stranger, whom Adamski named "Orthon," appeared. Supposedly they communicated through a combination of gestures and mental telepathy as Adamski's six companions watched this encounter from a distance. Adamski called this visit "truly the greatest experience that ever happened to me in my sixty-two years of earthly life." Surface thinkers, he said, would call it a hoax or a dream, but he questioned how they would explain the thousands of sightings over recent years and the six witnesses who would support his story.

Meanwhile, in England, an electronics expert by the name of Desmond Leslie was seeking a publisher for his book about the history of UFOs and interpretive ideas from nineteenth-century theosophy (teachings about God and the world based on mystical insight). A London publisher thought of packaging Leslie's manuscript with another shorter piece—Adamski's account, ghostwritten by Clara L. John, of his experiences with UFOs. This mismatched combination was published as *Flying Saucers Have Landed*, with Leslie and Adamski listed as co-authors. First published in 1953, it soon hit the bestseller list and fueled a new surge of interest in UFOs. Some have argued that this book marked a culture shift in perspective about UFOs (from science fiction to mythology) and that this book "launched many UFO cults."

In 1955, in a new book called *Inside the Space Ships*, ghostwritten by Charlotte Blodget, Adamski updated his followers on his adventures since his first contact with Orthon. He reported a visit with two men from Mars and Saturn and a second visit with Orthon, who introduced him to many technological wonders and to members of the "whole brotherhood of the Universe" who travel extensively throughout the universe to "see, first hand, a little more of the 'many mansions' in the Father's house to which your Bible refers."

Adamski told of being taken up into a spaceship several more times over the next few years. During one contact, he rode past the moon, which he reported had air, clouds, vegetation, trees, animals, and people. He witnessed life on Venus on another excursion; his "space brothers" threw him a party on still another trip. Adamski reported being "overcome with gratitude to our Divine Father for permitting His children from other worlds who understood our problems of Earth to come our way and extend helping hands of love and compassion to us." An old master space brother told him that a new age is beginning when Earth people learn that "God is not in some far distant place, but ever near in all manifestations, and within Man himself."

During this time, groups that had organized for objective research on UFOs began to uncover the truth about some of the so-called contactees. They contended that only a lunatic could believe these fantastic contactee stories. The best known of the contactees, Adamski naturally bore the most criticism; most people dismissed his excursions as fakes. One journalist said Adamski's best picture of a UFO was actually the "top of a canister-type vacuum cleaner," while someone else thought it was "the top of an ordinary chicken brooder" with three infrared brooder bulbs attached to the bottom to represent landing gear. A third critic noticed an "uncanny resemblance to electric light fittings with table tennis balls fixed underneath," and yet another recognized it as a Chrysler hubcap attached to a coffee can with three ping-pong balls.

Regardless, Adamski was "a big hit on the lecture circuit"; he traveled extensively across the United States and Canada and in 1959 embarked on a trip around the world. He said later, "In every nation I visited I found wonderful men and women who are dedicated to seeking out the peaceful, productive means by which we shall earn our rightful, dignified position among the civilizations of other planets." From the many people worldwide who wrote to him, Adamski organized the International Get Acquainted Program, groups that exchanged information and discussed Adamski's newsletters.

In 1961, when Lucy McGinnis resigned as Adamski's unpaid secretary and withdrew from the group, his coworkers noticed that his newsletters became shorter and often confusing. As Adamski himself admitted, McGinnis obviously "had been responsible for the clear formulation of [his] ideas."

Also that year Adamski published *Flying Saucers Farewell,* edited by C. A. Honey and reprinted in 1967 as *Behind the Flying Saucer Mystery.* Adamski included numerous biblical references in this book because, he said, "Our Bible contains several hundred reports of space visitations, all of which have been misinterpreted and misunderstood until recent years." He claimed that space people are "better Christians than we are. We have never believed in the teachings of Jesus. [We] kept the label [but] never lived Christ's teachings."

Armed with mounting evidence against Adamski's claims, many of his coworkers abandoned him. Some believed that he experienced the initial contact in the desert but fabricated the rest of his story. Others said that new aliens deceived and lied to him or that U.S. government agents purposely misled him with false information in order to discredit him. Honey suspected that the "new boys," whom he also called "negative space people," confused Adamski with hypnotically suggested ideas. Lucy McGinnis believed in the first contact in the desert, but she suspected Adamski made up stories about trips into space to compensate for a bruised ego when some followers left him. Still another version claims that when Adamski revealed some secret that the ETs had told him, they fed him false information to discredit him and protect themselves.

Sociologist David Stupple studied Adamski and concluded that he invented his stories and then grew to believe them himself. "Like many other utopians, he created a democratic world free of religious and racial prejudice in which, through good works and evolution, the individual could rise to the top." Stupple believes that living in a relatively isolated place and being supported by a group of followers allowed Adamski to create and maintain his own world. As is generally true for cult members, attacks by outsiders only confirmed their beliefs about a world gone amuck, in danger of destruction.

By 1963, the Adamski group was in disarray. In 1964, Lou Zinsstag, the leader of his study group in Switzerland, wrote to some coworkers that she was leaving. "I have never been asked to and never made a pledge to be a 'follower' of George Adamski, the kind he now seems to be looking for.... I have never believed *in* George Adamski, I only believed—for quite some time—what he has told me. And I still believe what he wrote in his books. But he now wants coworkers who implicitly believe in him like in God. This is something I can't do."

Characteristic of the mixed reactions he had earned throughout his life, news reports following his death in 1965 said, "When he died, he was still the object of great reverence, vilification and controversy"; he was "a talented dreamer who got it wrong; a man of too little education and too much imagination, reacting to a burdened, fast changing world." Adamski's longtime follower and friend Lucy McGinnis summarized his life: "He wanted brotherhood—that was the depth of his philosophy. He was a very kindly and deeply sincere man, but he had a tremendous ego." Although she had left the group, she still believed that he met an alien in the desert. "I was a witness," she said, "to his first contact, remember, and I could never denounce that which I know to be true."

The UFO Phenomenon

Adamski was not alone in his interest in UFOs. Speculation about UFOs began in the United States during World War II, when many military pilots reported strange lights that hovered beside their aircraft for a while before speeding away. Nicknamed "foo-fighters," they were generally dismissed as optical illusions.

The UFO sighting by Adamski and others in 1946 occurred almost a year before a more famous sighting further north. On June 24, 1947, Kenneth Arnold was flying his small private plane near Mt. Rainier in Washington during daylight hours when he saw nine bright, flat objects zigzagging near the mountain peaks, traveling well over one thousand miles per hour. He told reporters the objects moved "like a saucer skipping across water," thus coining the term "flying saucer." Historians of the UFO phenomenon mark this occurrence as the beginning of modern ufology and the introduction of the flying saucer as a significant part of North American popular culture.

Reports from Adamski and others from around the world, many from "unimpeachable sources," soon followed Arnold's sighting. Interest grew in January, 1948, when Captain Thomas Mantell, an Air National Guard pilot, died in a plane crash while chasing a metallic object "tremendous in size" over Louisville, Kentucky. The official explanation was that, thinking it a UFO, he followed an Air Force balloon upward until he lost consciousness from lack of oxygen.

The period from 1949 to 1951 saw much uncertainty among ufologists. The Air Force reorganized and increased its investigations of UFO reports while publicly claiming that most sightings were hoaxes or natural phenomena. Many suspected the Air Force was trying to cover up the truth.

In July of 1952, national interest was again stimulated when UFOs appeared for several hours three nights in a row over Washington, D.C. Donald Keyhoe, a well-known UFO observer, wrote dramatically, "Until tonight some had laughed off the idea of visitors from other planets. But now they were badly shaken . . . for the simultaneous radar tracks and visual sightings added up to only one answer. Up there in the night some kind of super machines were reconnoitering the capital . . . plainly guided by highly intelligent beings."

By 1956, the U.S. government said that it could identify all but .4 percent of sightings as natural phenomena or "auto-suggestive myths." But contactees accused the U.S. Air Force and other government agencies of a "conspiracy of silence." They suspected the government was covering up evidence that the UFOs were indeed piloted by aliens, classifying evidence as intelligence information. Even many who were not part of the contactee subculture admitted that too many sightings had occurred to dismiss them all as fakes, mental aberrations, or natural phenomena. Government investigations unearthed many cases that could not be explained in any of these ways.

During the fifties, Hollywood films began to include more encounters with aliens, and the popularity of these films contributed to the confusion of fact and fiction. Although all contactees described aliens as good and kind, most of the early films, with titles such as *Invasion of the Body Snatchers* and *Invaders from Mars*, portrayed the aliens as evil invaders come to conquer the earth. One exception was *The Day the Earth Stood Still*, which tells of a flying saucer landing in Washington, D.C., with an alien who unsuccessfully tries to convince the people of Earth to stop their wars.

By the end of the fifties, people were losing interest in stories of contacts with aliens, and even UFO groups were dismissing them as false. Before long, however, a new myth emerged in the form of the abductee phenomenon. The abductees painted a darker, less positive picture of the alien visitors. The case of Betty and Barney Hill especially created widespread interest. In 1961, after returning home to New Hampshire from a vacation in Canada, the Hills were both troubled by strange dreams and a missing two-hour period on the way home. Undergoing hypnosis, they remembered that they had been abducted and taken aboard a UFO, where they underwent physical examinations. A book about their experience, *Interrupted Journey*, became a best-seller, and a film followed. This and many following similar stories introduced a new myth that aliens are visiting Earth to perform experiments on humans.

As contactees portrayed a more negative picture of aliens, the movie industry moved in the opposite direction, introducing highly popular films showing aliens as mystical, benevolent, and human in appearance, often teaching a New Age philosophy. Steven Spielberg's 1977 *Close Encounters of the Third Kind* was certainly among the most influential, but many others have followed, including *ET, Batteries Not Included, Starman, Enemy Mine,* and *Cocoon.*

Reports of UFOs spread rapidly around the world during the eighties and nineties. Jacques Vallee, a diligent investigator who tries to approach UFOs from a scientific perspective, estimates that the number of sightings are now in the millions. Gallup Polls now show that about half of Americans believe in UFOs, about 25 percent believe they come from outer space, and more than one in ten say that they have seen something that could be a UFO. After years of research, Vallee concluded UFOs are real, although he does not know what they are or where they come from. More and more people are similarly concluding that something is going on that cannot be explained as swamp gas, fraud, or hallucination. When asked if the government is covering up the truth, Vallee says officials don't know anything to cover up.

"Space Brothers" Theology

To Adamski and many of his followers, UFOs and alien visits are more than interesting natural phenomena. "Space brothers" theology, closely akin with the New Age movement, has invaded our culture.

Adamski's Monistic View

As Adamski clearly indicated in his first book, *Wisdom of the Masters of the Far East,* his theology was based on *monism.* If God is All, it follows that we are God, or part of God, or an expression of God—"that diamond chip which is identical with the great diamond." But humanity has fallen. To Adamski that meant we have become separated from the God-Universe. The only gift of God is our human potential. God is passive and "will wait billions of years for man to will himself back to being part of the whole." Like so many others, he believed that at death the soul moves through reincarnation to rebirth in other forms, both on the earth and in "other planes."

Adamski distinguished between Jesus and The Christ. To him, Jesus was, along with Confucius and Buddha, one of the Masters, one of the Illuminati, "one who is actually living 'in the image and likeness' of the Father and therefore is wholly impersonal, with no feeling of separation or division." A Master is said to be a manifestation in human form of The Christ. To Adamski, "I and the Father are one," was

Jesus' most important teaching, and he interpreted it to mean that Jesus understood and accepted the principle of monism. To him, The Christ is a unifying force or intelligence in the universe. Adamski said, "In our present state we cannot receive the full light of God. The Christ is the intermediary between God and man, the transformer which reduces the Total Power to the proper volume acceptable to each particular channel." To have Christ within us means to be willing to turn from self and serve the "Universal Principle," thereby establishing the Kingdom of Heaven on earth.

Adamski also rejected the distinction between good and evil; opposites are contrary to unity. He thought the only sin is ignorance; the greatest sin is ignorance of one's own perfection. What we call *wickedness* is merely a "misapplication" of universal principles that needs to be corrected. Humanity has fallen in the sense of losing its balance; in the process it has lost its place as part of God. He considered even the distinction between male and female to be part of a fallen state—presumably a return to unity would end this distinction. Neither does he recognize any inherent necessity that one becomes ill or grows old, since both spring from ignorance. He saw a need for a process of gradual growth and purification through a release from personal goals and desires and an increasing devotion to service of the All.

UFOs and the New Age Movement

Many people see no connection between UFOs and the New Age movement. Of course, seeing a UFO or even thinking one has been abducted by an alien does not make a person a New Ager. On the other hand, a New Ager usually does not dismiss UFOs or alien visits as an insignificant curiosity.

The interests of UFO followers and New Agers are hardly distinguishable. Both accept reincarnation, holistic health, one-world government, continuing evolution, psychic abilities, rejection of the distinction between good and evil, monism, and denial that Jesus was the Christ. In recent years the UFO movement has been shifting toward a more psychic and religious emphasis, difficult to distinguish from the New Age movement.

Many New Age channelers, including Shirley MacLaine (see chapter 5), believe in UFOs. The term *channeling* originated with contactees and spread to those who formerly were called *mediums* or *spiritualists*. People now report receiving messages from aliens through trance, automatic writing, clairvoyance, mental telepathy, space beams, intuition, hunches, and abductions.

Abductions have captured center stage in the UFO subculture, and most researchers now focus on this phenomenon. In 1987, Whitley

Strieber reported in his best-seller *Communion* that he had been abducted by aliens. He described his experience as "hell on earth," and the aliens as menacing, sinister, and monstrously ugly, reminding him of the "legendary cunning of demons." Researcher John Whitmore found that "aliens perform many of the traditional functions of God. They create humanity, guide it through history, and eventually offer a form of salvation, all through a nearly omnipotent technology that replaces the miraculous will of God for modern humankind."

Growing numbers of UFO enthusiasts accept that hundreds of thousands of aliens are among us, walking about in human bodies. A walk-in is described as a "highly developed discarnate entity who takes over the body and personality of an incarnate adult in order to work to raise spiritual consciousness" and thus help us through the troubled times in which we live. Ruth Montgomery popularized this belief in *Strangers Among Us*, which claims that Jesus Christ "surrendered to a walk-in" at his baptism.

In his 1991 book, *UFOs in the New Age,* William Alnor says that after traveling twenty thousand miles interviewing people and attending conferences, he concluded that the UFO movement has "blossomed into a powerful religious movement. It has an apocalyptic bent; the aliens usually say they have something to do with the end times referred to in the Bible, and many talk about a 'second coming.'" By comparison, religions like Mormonism and Scientology are not far from teachings of the contactees and abductees of the UFO movement which have also found their way into New Age beliefs. Jacques Vallee says that Joseph Smith, the founder of Mormonism, who in 1820 saw a pillar of light and "two Personages whose brightness and glory defy all description," would be considered a contactee if he had his vision today. Alnor points out that Ron Hubbard's idea of spiritual Thetans evolving through millions of years, moving from one body or galaxy to another, also incorporates some themes consistent with ufology (see the next chapter in this study for a discussion of Ron Hubbard's Scientology).

UFO Cults

The UFO movement is divided, although not always very clearly, between those interested in collecting scientific evidence about UFOs and those with a more religious approach. Those with a religious approach often become members of a cult, a religious group whose beliefs and practices vary significantly from those of the established religions of society. "Seekers" commonly move restlessly from one group to another. Many of these groups are short-lived, but new groups form constantly. (Under the heading of "Flying Saucer

Groups," the *Encyclopedia of American Religions* lists twenty different groups, including the George Adamski Foundation.)

Much of what these groups teach can already be found in Theosophy and various other spiritualist groups of the nineteenth century. Although their beliefs differ somewhat, the common patterns run something like this:

- A difficult time of cleansing is coming to the earth during which people must either shift to a new way of thinking or be eliminated.

- The new age will introduce "Christ consciousness." People will become "christed" and develop physical abilities that Jesus showed after his resurrection and will continue to evolve and travel throughout the universe.

Because of such beliefs, UFO cults have been described as the apocalyptic branch of the New Age.

J. Gordon Melton says, "Contactees . . . should be approached as participants in an occult religious movement. They are not kooks, but they are people who have been swept into a movement because of a direct experience with some extraordinary occurrence. These experiences resemble most closely common visionary and psychic experiences cast in a framework of space age technology."

Questions for the Christian

As we have noted, merely sighting a UFO does not indicate belief in Adamski's or the New Age theology. But how does the Christian explain UFOs and space aliens?

Something Strange Out There?

Because the term *UFO* covers a great range of phenomena, more than one explanation for their appearance is likely. An estimated 95 percent of sightings can be explained as natural phenomena, yet many investigators are saying "something strange is out there" that is neither hoax nor physical object. Four theories are presently being advanced to explain these strange UFOs.

- **Geophysical Explanations**
  Researchers have proposed that stresses along geological fault lines could result in unusual electrically-charged gases in the air, causing strange lights, body burns, unconsciousness, machine malfunction, and lightbulb failure. This stress could also possibly influence the human brain, causing disorientation and hallucinations.

- **Psychological Explanations**
  Another theory suggests that some who report UFOs may suffer

from serious mental problems. They often reveal these stories under hypnosis. Abductees commonly trace their first encounters back to early childhood, and they often report stressful childhood experiences. Others supposedly suffer from an "emotional and intellectual crisis" and are probably more prone than average to escapism and fantasy, using UFOs to relieve anxieties and give meaning to the universe and their own lives.

- **An Intrusion of a Different Dimension**
  Some researchers and abductees maintain that UFOs are "dimensional interface phenomena," which assumes the existence of a parallel universe or another dimension to reality that we ordinarily cannot experience. This universe contains beings, perhaps supernatural, that are now encroaching on our world.

- **A Human Conspiracy**
  Jacques Vallee says in *Messengers of Deception* that "UFOs . . . are an application of psychotronic technology . . . physical devices used to affect human consciousness" to achieve "systematic manipulation of witnesses and contactees. . . . And the data [his research] suggest that the manipulators may be human beings with a plan for social control."

Angels or Demons?

The topic of angels is very popular among New Agers today. To Adamski, aliens coming in UFOs are like guardian angels, and many today in the UFO subculture claim regular contact with angels.

Billy Graham would not, of course, agree with Adamski's views, but he does lean toward the idea that UFOs are angels. In *Angels: God's Secret Agents* he contends that although this is all speculative, "UFOs are astonishingly angel-like in some of their reported appearances." Yet other Christians believe that the UFO aliens are fallen angels, working under Satan, demonic forces that manipulate both human minds and physical matter. Some believe they are a portend of the last days and the coming of the anti-Christ. Certainly, as we have seen in the case of Adamski, the messages reported by contactees and abductees are often anti-Christian; this suggests their source, if indeed supernatural rather than psychological, is demonic rather than angelic.

Extraterrestrial Beings?

Theologians and philosophers have debated the question of ETs since antiquity. Billy Graham says, "I firmly believe there are intelligent beings like us far away in space who worship God . . . they are God's creation." David Wimbish in his book *Something's Going On Out*

There says, "God isn't wasteful, and since He created all the planets and stars of the universe, it wouldn't surprise me at all if he put living creatures on many of them. . . . But my faith in Christ would take precedence over anything the space being might say."

Space-age theology challenges the Christian to test the spirits. If they are from God, they will acknowledge the lordship of Jesus Christ. In fact, in most reports the aliens explicitly deny Jesus' lordship, teaching instead a New Age monism.

Suggestions for Group Session

Getting Started

Welcome new participants to your group and spend a few minutes sharing individual perceptions of the New Age movement gained from the previous session's discussion. You may want to focus on the influence of monism in our popular culture and highlight any examples that members of your group have noticed since you last met.

Flying saucers and space people are part of our everyday fare—on everything from packaging for toys to the toys themselves, from advertising on television and radio to the programs on the airwaves and big screen, and from the eyes of the imaginative and scientific to the hearts of religious cults.

Maybe some of us can say with David Wimbish that "God created all the living creatures, and it wouldn't hurt my faith a single bit if a flying saucer landed on the White House lawn one of these days." Perhaps some of us have unanswered questions about UFOs and alien visitors from space and are more inclined to agree with J. Gordon Melton: "Contactees . . . should be approached as participants in an occult religious movement."

Whatever our interest in UFOs and our "comfort zone" with the scientific aspects of this phenomenon, we are challenged to weigh the beliefs and practices of the space-age theologians to see if they are from God. God himself tells us how to do this with his command at the Transfiguration as recorded in Mark 9:7: "This is my Son, whom I love. Listen to him!"

Begin this session with this prayer:

Many and great, O God, are your works,
Maker of earth and sky;
Your hands have set the heavens with stars;
Your fingers spread the mountains and plains.
You merely spoke and waters were formed;
Deep seas obey your voice.

Grant us communion with you, our God,
Though you transcend the stars.
Come close to us and stay by our side:
With you are found the true gifts that last.
Bless us with life which never shall end,
Eternal life with you.
—"Many and Great," Words: Joseph R. Renville,
© 1846; translated by Philip Frazier, 1929

(If you wish to sing the prayer, the words and music are included in *Songs for Life,* 94 and *Presbyterian Hymnal,* 271.)

Group Discussion and Activity

1. Read Romans 1:18-20, 25. How is it possible that someone like Adamski, who acquired from his parents "an unusual and deeply religious approach to the wonders of creation," came to worship the "created things rather than the Creator"? Could this worship of the created things invade our space-age explorations or our environmental concerns?

2. Read Exodus 25:8; 1 Kings 8:27; and Ephesians 3:16-17. How would you respond to Adamski's claim that "an old master space brother told him that a new age is beginning" when Earth people will learn that "God is not in some far distant place, but ever near in all manifestations, and within Man himself"?

3. Among the "several hundred reports of space visitations" Adamski claims are found in the Bible are John 8:23; 14:3 (which Adamski say prove that Jesus was from outer space) and Acts 1:9 (by which he claims that Jesus entered a spaceship when he ascended). What do these passages tell Christians?

4. Read John 8:12-18, 24. How do these verses collide with Adamski's monistic view that Jesus is just one of the "Masters" with "no feeling of separation or division" from the Father?

5. Adamski claimed space people exist and "are better Christians than we are." Whether or not we believe this, are we guilty of his accusation, "We have never believed in the teachings of Jesus . . . never lived Christ's teachings"?

6. At one point Adamski said Wall Street "would like nothing better than to have this whole thing (UFOs) thrown into the field of the psychic, called a cult, and discredited in the minds of sincere people." What evidence do you find woven throughout Adamski's life

and the New Age UFO movement that would convince you that Wall Street could be right?

7. How do Hollywood films and their portrayal of "mystical, benevolent, and human" aliens appeal to children and teenagers? What is the danger that these films will teach New Age philosophy? Can we accept entertainment that is anti-Christ?

8. What is your answer to each of the three questions for the Christian raised in this chapter? Read 1 John 4:1-6 as you formulate your answers.

Closing

Think about this description of our world today from this "testimony of faith for our times."

Rebel cries sound through the world:
some, crushed by failure
or hardened by pain,
give up on life and hope and God;
others, shaken,
but still hoping for human triumph,
work feverishly to realize their dreams.
As believers in God
we join this struggle of the spirits,
testing our times by the Spirit's sure Word.
—*Our World Belongs to God*, 3

Close this session with a prayer of thanksgiving and praise: God is King! Let the earth be glad! Ask for God's Spirit to lead us in his truth.

THREE

SCIENTOLOGY ORGANIZED BY L. RON HUBBARD

Hubbard's Journey to New Age

L. Ron Hubbard has been called charming, dynamic, creative, a great leader, a charismatic genius, and one of this century's most important and influential authors. He's also been called predatory, paranoid, schizophrenic, a megalomaniac, and the greatest con artist who ever lived. Whatever else he was, Hubbard was clearly an exceptional storyteller, and by far the most interesting story he told was about himself. This story can teach us a lot about New Age thinking.

Early Influences

Growing up on his grandfather's enormous cattle ranch in Montana, Hubbard spent most of his time outdoors with cowboys and Native Americans. He was the youngest Eagle Scout in the country and during his teenage years was made a blood brother to the Blackfoot nation. With the financial support of his indulgent grandfather, he traveled extensively, sitting at the feet of holy men in the Far East. During these travels he became interested in the spiritual destiny of humanity.

While studying nuclear physics at George Washington University, he earned a reputation as a skilled and daring barnstorming pilot. Soon after, he became a member of the Explorers Club and went on expeditions in Alaskan, Caribbean, and Atlantic waters. He was awarded the prestigious Explorer's Club flag. At the age of twenty, he directed the Caribbean Motion Picture Expedition and the next year led the first mineralogical survey of Puerto Rico. These experiences later qualified him for service with the Navy.

Career Paths

In 1932, following his trip to Puerto Rico and with an academic record suggesting little chance of graduation, Hubbard dropped out of college. He made a precarious living as a writer of adventure stories for pulp magazines. These magazines were popular during the Great Depression, offering a cheap form of escape into adventures of heroic men defeating their evil enemies and rescuing beautiful women.

In 1937, Hubbard's first book-length novel, *Buckskin Brigades,* was published. By 1938, established as a top-selling adventure story writer and favorably compared with H. G. Wells and Edgar Allan Poe, he became a "legend among legends," greatly admired by his fellow writers. At the same time, he became a successful Hollywood screenwriter. In 1940, *Final Blackout,* one of his most popular novels and still available in bookstores, was published.

Before the outbreak of World War II, Hubbard was called into service as a naval officer. By the end of the war, he was a much-decorated hero, wounded seriously several times. Russell Miller in *Bare-Faced Messiah* records Hubbard's account of his death on the operating table during the war as retold by his literary agent:

> *Basically what he told me was that after he died he rose in spirit form. . . . He could see a kind of intellectual smorgasbord on which was outlined everything that had ever puzzled the mind of man. All the questions that had concerned philosophers through the ages . . . were there answered. All this information came flooding into him, and while he was absorbing it, there was a sort of flustering in the air, and he felt something like a long umbilical cord pulling him back. He was saying, "No, no, not yet!" but he was pulled back anyway. . . . According to Ron, (when he regained consciousness) he jumped off the operating table, ran to his Quonset hut, got two reams of paper and a gallon of scalding black coffee and for the next forty-eight hours, at a blinding rate, he wrote a work called* Excalibur.

Although Hubbard's naval records mention no wounds, blindness, operations, or miraculous recoveries, Hubbard claimed he was miraculously cured from his various injuries through techniques later developed into Scientology. Later he claimed he had written *Excalibur* in 1938, prior to his navy tale, but the book was never published, and there is no evidence that anyone ever saw a manuscript.

At the end of the war, Hubbard met John Whiteside Parsons, a well-known scientist and follower of Aleister Crowley. Crowley, the English author of *The Book of the Law*, taught, "Do what thou wilt shall be the whole of the Law." Crowley claimed that a "messenger from the forces ruling this Earth at present" dictated this book to him in 1904 and that he was the beast in the book of Revelation. Hubbard's son later claimed that his father considered himself Crowley's successor, the rightful heir to the "Throne of the Beast." Bent Croydon (in *L. Ron Hubbard, Messiah or Madman?* co-authored with Hubbard's son) argues that many of Hubbard's later writings were "simply rehashings of data and techniques from the writings of Aleister Crowley."

Hubbard soon became involved in Parson's Pasadena, California, chapter of Crowley's organization, Ordo Templi Orientis, which practiced magical sexual rituals. It's uncertain to what extent Hubbard believed in Satanism and magic, but he apparently convinced Parsons that he was sincere and was "in direct touch with some higher intelligence." (Scientologists later claimed Hubbard was working undercover for naval intelligence to expose this group.)

During the period from 1947 to 1950, Hubbard transformed from fiction writer to religious leader. Speaking at a writer's convention, Hubbard uttered his most quoted words: "Writing for a penny a word is ridiculous. If a man really wants to make a million dollars, the best way would be to start his own religion."

During this period, word began to spread among science fiction fans that Hubbard was working on a new "science of the mind." In January 1950, the famous columnist Walter Winchell announced: "There is something new coming up in April called Dianetics, a new science which works with the invariability of physical science in the field of the human mind. From all indications, it will prove to be as revolutionary for humanity as the first caveman's discovery and utilization of fire" (Miller).

In the May 1950, issue of *Astounding*, with considerable advance editorial support from Campbell, Hubbard's "new" ideas first appeared in an article entitled "Dianetics: A New Science of the Mind." Spurred by readers' great interest, he produced *Dianetics: The Modern Science of Mental Health*. With the introduction of Dianetics and Scientology, Hubbard is said to have contributed the most important advance in the understanding of the mind since Freud.

A New Age Leader

The fad of Dianetics exploded in 1950; in July the book appeared on best-seller lists. People across the United States bought the book and tried it out on their friends. "Dianetics parties" became common in some areas. Although a few medical doctors and scientists wrote glowing testimonies for Dianetics, most professional journals of medicine, psychology, and psychiatry either ignored it or condemned it as dangerous. Nor did all science fiction writers approve; one called it "gibberish" and another a "lunatic revision of Freudian psychology."

Meanwhile the Hubbard Dianetic Research Foundation of Elizabeth, New Jersey, emerged to continue the development of Dianetics. Before long, however, Hubbard and his partners disagreed on a variety of issues. Hubbard moved on to form new organizations in Los Angeles, Wichita, and finally to form the beginnings of the Church of Scientology in Phoenix in 1953. During this time and following two previous marriages, Hubbard married Mary Sue Whipp, who was to play a leading role in Scientology.

Scientology's central teaching is that the human body is a temporary home for a spirit being called a *thetan*. Scientology's goal is to free spiritual beings from the material universe in which they have been trapped, releasing them from suffering and unhappiness. The ultimate goal of Scientology, according to Hubbard, is to "clear the planet," to eliminate the reactive mind in each person. This would bring "total freedom" and end all our problems.

Hubbard grew wealthy as a leader of the growing New Age religion—thousands admired, feared, and almost worshipped him. Ron and Mary Sue moved to England to a large country estate to head the Hubbard Association of Scientology International. Over the years, Hubbard lectured to upper-level members and wrote twenty books on Dianetics and Scientology. He also gained much publicity from a photo of himself with an E-meter attached to a tomato plant, demonstrating that plants have emotions.

Although Scientology was growing and taking in millions, Hubbard found himself in trouble with government agencies in various countries. The public opinion of Scientology was changing from "just another self-improvement group" to "dangerous cult." Scientologists began to perceive themselves as a persecuted religion. In 1967, at the age of fifty-six, after spending millions of dollars in a failed attempt to establish himself as a leading figure in Rhodesia in order to find a safe base for Scientology, Hubbard officially resigned as president of the church. He began the Sea Org (Sea Organization), a small private navy of a few ships and three- to four-hundred members with himself as commodore. Scientologists were told that the Sea Org was a "regathering of loyal officers" from a 75-million-year-old battle to clear the planet. The public was told that Hubbard had returned to his previous interest in exploring.

In the confined atmosphere of life at sea, the Sea Org became the whole life of its members, who were required to sign a million-year contract. Many expected to be sent to other worlds after the earth was fully "cleared" and made a "Scientology planet." Their horizons often narrowed to exclude competing ideas, and they became what some have called *rondroids*. Croydon reports that Scientology became "a place where ministers dress in military uniforms and scream profanities . . . [and] a dear and close friend may, at the flick of an 'ethics order,' become an evil being never to be communicated with again." People who questioned or added to Hubbard's "tech" came to be called *squirrels,* and posters urged, "Stamp Out Squirrels."

Since Hubbard spent much of his time in his cabin hiding from possible enemies (called *SPs* for "suppressive persons"), some of the teenage children of committed Scientologists were given the privilege of waiting on Hubbard. They communicated his orders, ran errands, lighted his cigarettes, cleaned his clothing, and helped him dress. They came to be known as the *CMO* (Commodore's Messenger Organization). From the early seventies to the end of his life, the CMO waited on Hubbard constantly. Because Hubbard's orders came more and more through the CMO, these young people, many with little formal education, gained increasing power in the organization.

In 1975 the Sea Org sold the ships and established new headquarters in Clearwater, Florida. Around this time, Hubbard launched a series of secret and sometimes illegal operations to protect Scientology and discredit its critics. In the best known of these, "Operation Snow White," members infiltrated government agencies to gain access to and alter files on Scientology and Hubbard. This led to massive FBI raids on Scientology centers around the country and eventually to the conviction of nine leaders of Scientology, including Mary Sue Hubbard.

In 1980 Hubbard disappeared. It was unclear whether orders were coming from Hubbard or from the CMO, because from 1980 until his death all communications came through three members of the CMO. During this period many longtime members were forced out of leadership positions under impossible demands to find more "raw meat" (new members) and increase income (reportedly running at about a million dollars a week). Croydon states that "the top executives and personalities of Scientology, some six hundred people who had given the most important youthful years of their lives to work ridiculous hours for the cause, were now officially declared to be evil psychotic beings."

David Miscavige, one of the three leading CMOs, reported Hubbard's death to a gathering of Scientologists in the Hollywood Palladium. According to Miller, Miscavige said:

> On January 25, 1986, "L. Ron Hubbard discarded the body he had used in this lifetime for seventy-four years. . . . [It] had ceased to be useful and in fact had become an impediment to the work he now must do outside its confines. The being we knew as L. Ron Hubbard still exists. . . . He has simply moved on to his next step. LRH in fact used this lifetime and body we knew to accomplish what no man has ever accomplished—he unlocked the mysteries of life and gave us the tools so we could free ourselves and our fellow men."

What Is Scientology?

Science Fiction Religion

Scientology has been called "the first science fiction religion" because some of the themes of science fiction carry over into the religious beliefs. Ingo Morth, writing in *Social Compass*, specifically described Scientology as a religion offering "concrete behavioral guidelines and techniques . . . promising the transgression of limitations and life's problems . . . on the basis of ideas developed within the science fiction branch of literature."

A strong religious element seems almost inevitable in an account of a fictional society set in the future or in some far-off galaxy. A comprehensive overview of how such a society functions without explaining its religion—its answers to ultimate questions, its basic values, and its forms of worship or lack thereof—would be impossible. Often ancient religions, particularly Buddhism and Hinduism, help construct these fictional religions. At the same time, Christianity is portrayed as a reflection of limited human experience needing replacement with something that can include thousands of other life forms in the universe—each, possibly, with a religion of its own. This easily leads to monism—the "all is one" view, the central theme of New Age thinking.

The most notable example of the science fiction emphasis came in 1961 with the publication of Robert Heinlein's *Stranger in a Strange Land*. Full of New Age theology, it is called "the most famous science fiction novel ever written" and is especially popular in New Age circles. For example, the hero of this story comes from Mars to Earth to teach people "Thou art God, and I am God." He claims to be teaching "simply a method of efficient functioning," not a faith.

The common theme of people meeting aliens tends toward a view of humanity as only a tiny segment of all the intelligent life-forms in the universe. Alien space travelers from the past may have brought Christianity and other religions to earth. With the requisite understanding, time and space limitations are surmountable, and humankind in the near future will enter a better, more advanced form either socially or physically. In a society that has overcome war and poverty, highly intelligent people can communicate mentally, without speech.

The Dianetics Stage

Science fiction fan-club members provided a "continuous feedback process" to science fiction writers and by the late forties expected a new breakthrough in the "science of the mind." That Hubbard's ideas would appear first in a science fiction magazine did not seem strange to them. Hubbard gave voice to their "dream of a utopia supported by the powers of science and technology, a utopia characterized by personal, rather than social, gratification . . . available in practice only to an 'elect,' to the 'right sort of people'" (Albert Berger, in *Science-Fiction Studies*).

Although science fiction, general semantics, and many other sources have been suggested for Dianetics, probably the most important source was Sigmund Freud. Thomas Gutheil, professor of psychiatry at Harvard Medical School, said in the July 6, 1992, issue of *Time:*

> *Freud took two pieces of Vermont folk wisdom and turned them into a science. The first was, "There's a whole lot more to folks than meets the eye." This became known as the theory of the unconscious. The second was, "Keep your mouth shut, and you might learn something." He changed the position of the doctor from that of an authoritarian giving orders to a more receptive role. Freud said, "Let the patient talk and tell the story."*

Hubbard taught that mind has three parts:

- an analytic part that perfectly records all experience and operates much like a computer unless some trauma upsets it,
- a reactive part that stores *engrams*, disturbing memories of emotionally or physically painful experiences,
- and a somatic part that carries out the directions of the analytic mind on the physical level.

He asserted that most mental problems and many physical problems are caused by engrams, some of which go back as far as the fetal stage.

Dianetics claims that one's physical and mental health can be improved through a process called *auditing* (listening), in which engrams are erased from the reactive mind and stored in the analytic mind where they can be dealt with rationally. Auditors (therapists) are trained to use a highly structured method of directing the attention through various commands and questions to help a person remember and defuse disturbing events by "running" them (reliving them in detail). Later, Hubbard introduced an instrument called an E-meter (electrometer) to aid in auditing. This skin galvanometer resembles those used by some psychologists and in lie detectors, although its purpose was to aid in locating engrams.

Followers claimed that this process could cure a variety of ills (severe depression, schizophrenia, backache, stuttering, sinus problems, and poor eyesight); improve memory; raise intelligence significantly; and make one more creative, successful, and happy. A person freed of all engrams would be fully rational and without error. Hubbard wrote in *Dianetics*, "Man is good. Take away his basic aberrations and with them go the evil of which the scholastic and the moralist were so fond. The only detachable portion of him is the 'evil' portion. And when it is detached, his personality and vigor intensify."

The appeal of Dianetics has been attributed by some to Hubbard's abilities as a confidence trickster. This seems at best an oversimplification. Miller provides this explanation:

> *The dismissal of people interested in Dianetics as a "lunatic fringe" is not helpful or accurate. There is no evidence that people attracted to Dianetics differed significantly from average. Many realized that Hubbard was far from perfect, but they had faith in what they saw as his discovery of a new and superior technique. One follower later reported, "Maybe he was a charlatan and a liar—I didn't care. The point was that the tech [technology] was good. It worked."*

Hubbard failed to produce clear people with superior intelligence and total recall. Dianetics soon faded from popular interest. Many who first had high hopes for Dianetics abandoned Hubbard when they noticed movement from a strictly scientific approach to something that resembled a religious or occult practice.

The Introduction of Scientology

As interest in Dianetics faded, Hubbard announced he had made new discoveries that built upon but exceeded Dianetics. In what he would call *Scientology,* people being audited reported experiences not only from the womb but from past lives. The E-meter seemed to confirm that people were telling the truth about remembering experiences in medieval Europe or ancient Rome. Many gave accounts of flying saucers, space travel, and life on other planets; these memories, in fact, became an expected element of auditing. While Hubbard presented Dianetics as a self-improvement technique, Scientology was soon registered as a religion.

Scientology's central teaching focused on the *thetan,* the spirit being that lives in the human body as an individual expression of *theta,* the source of all life, the ground of all being. The thetan is immaterial and immortal, separate from the physical universe. Each thetan is its own god in the sense of being uncaused by anyone or anything else. Thetans created the material world, called *MEST* (matter, energy, space, and time), for their own entertainment. They became so involved with their own creation, however, that they are now confined within MEST and have developed a reactive mind full of engrams. The thetan no longer thinks entirely rationally, nor can it remember its past before it entered the present body.

The focus of Scientology is still on the removal of engrams. The added dimension is that engrams are said to be implanted not only by experiences in the present body but also by experiences in all other previously occupied bodies. Thousands upon thousands of these—both human, animal, and plant—extend back over trillions of years. A thetan could gain "total freedom" only by auditing all the engrams from every previous life. (Interestingly, this goal of total freedom is the same as that given by Aleister Crowley for the practice of magic.) Eventually a thetan could become free of a reactive mind and "exterior" to the body—an out-of-body experience. In this condition, the thetan would once more be an operating thetan (OT), rehabilitated to the god-like being it was before being captured by MEST.

This doctrine of Scientology is typical of the New Age emphasis on the superiority of the spiritual over the material. It also suggests the central teaching of the New Age movement—the monistic view that we are all a part of some great spiritual cosmic force or being. Harriet Whitehead in *Renunciation and Reformulation: A Study of Conversion of an American Sect* points out that similar "memories" of past lives are found in Freudian psychotherapy and also influenced Carl Jung, a hero of the New Age, in his development of the idea of a "collective unconscious."

Since spiritual beings have gotten themselves into the trap of the material world, no one else can help them. Each must solve his or her own problems (another common New Age theme). A savior is unnecessary, since salvation lies within each individual. In his book *Scientology,* Hubbard said that an operating thetan "goes through walls, barriers, vanishes space, appears anywhere at will and does other remarkable things. It must be, then, that an individual can be trapped only when he considers that he is trapped."

Over the years Hubbard added more steps considered necessary to achieve the goal of OT. The process is called "flowing up the bridge," because people were told that once they had made the initial "leap of faith" they were on "the bridge to total freedom." The bridge begins with total memory, then improvements in communication, then learning to take responsibility for one's own problems, then purging of engrams, then a freeing from "fixed ideas" (things that Scientology declares wrong). At this point one is considered ready for the higher levels of the bridge where, in an attempt to free oneself from MEST (the material universe), one emphasizes developing "OT powers" such as out-of-body experiences, telepathy, and telekinesis. Whitehead uses Scientology terminology to describe the highest level where people audit themselves (solo auditing):

> *Mystical states are reported; the sense of self suffusing the universe, the experience of reaching a point of blissful stillness, the sense of possessing vast ineffable knowledge. One unusual experience frequently reported, because commonly looked for, is the sensation of being out of one's body—the condition of "exteriorization."*

The higher levels of this "bridge" are considered so dangerous that one could die in attempting them without proper Scientology training. Critics suggest that a new level was revealed whenever income began to fall off.

In the sixties, Hubbard wove an elaborate story of the history of the universe, including a "galactic confrontation" in which overpopulation was solved by sending millions of thetans to earth. Here they were separated from their bodies by H-bombs 75 million years ago. (If this were true, from the millions killed we would expect to find a few 75-million-year-old human fossils today, but none have been discovered.) Hubbard taught that each human body today contains a whole cluster of these traumatized thetans (called *BTs* for body thetans) that must be removed through auditing if the dominant healthy thetan is to attain OT status. An ex-member reported, "I observed something very odd: The wealthier the Scientologist, the more 'body thetans' he had. . . . It is quite usual for Scientologists to spend well over $100,000 for this level alone. One man, a geologist, engineer, and entrepreneur, spent $450,000" (Croydon). The whole story has been described as a combination of exorcism with bad science fiction.

Hubbard's Church of Scientology does not fit the traditional view of a church. Although it has constructed chapels and holds occasional services, participation is optional. Thus Scientology seems to lack an important part of Christianity: common worship. This is not surprising, considering that its theology lacks the concept of a personal God. People do not gather to worship some ephemeral "theta," especially if they consider themselves to be part of the entity. Naturally, then, Scientology's major activity is working with the individual in auditing sessions.

Most people approach Scientology with a goal of improving their personal lives. Frequently they are offered a free personality test. Gradually they are introduced to the more religious aspects that merely seem to suggest further steps to self-development. A former Scientology member explains that when he was a member, he liked the feeling that he "had all the answers," but ultimately he was unsatisfied. He says, "I need something, someone, in my life" (*The Banner,* April 10, 1989). Scientology cannot offer someone, because it does not accept a personal god. Eventually, this man, after leaving Scientology, met a Christian Reformed chaplain in Toronto, who showed him that one doesn't need *all* the answers, only *the* answer. "In my studies I learned that doubting and questioning are normal for any thinking person. My studies satisfied me. I started to trust again. I believed that Jesus Christ is the Way, the Truth, and the Life."

Scientology After Hubbard

In the post-Hubbard era, the Church of Scientology, now led by David Miscavige, a second generation member who never finished high school, continues to tell his story of "total freedom." It has devoted much money and energy to advertising Hubbard and his book *Dianetics.* The church claims to have seven hundred centers in sixty-five countries and millions of members, but others estimate that, with its high turnover rate, the church has one hundred thousand or even fewer members.

A 1991 *Time* magazine report called Scientology a "hugely profitable global racket that survives by intimidating members and critics in a Mafia-like manner," and quotes the director of the Cult Awareness Network as saying, "Scientology is quite likely the most ruthless, the most classically terroristic, the most litigious and the most lucrative cult the country has ever seen."

Reports indicate that new and higher levels of auditing are offered at rates as high as one thousand dollars an hour. The *Time* magazine analysis found money is also being raised through new organizations that do not publicize their connection to Scientology. Two of these organizations offer human potential training to corporations. A description of their content sounds much like the early stages of Dianetics. Sterling Management Systems sends a free newsletter to three hundred thousand health-care professionals, promising to increase their incomes through seminars and courses costing thousands. HealthMed, a chain of clinics run by Scientology, promotes a system designed by Hubbard to "purify the body" with saunas, exercises, and vitamins. Narconon, another Scientology organization, controls thirty alcohol and drug rehabilitation centers, besides some in prisons under the name *Criminon.*

Time found other front-line organizations that work for Scientology goals. The Way to Happiness Foundations distributed over 3.5 million copies of a Hubbard booklet on morality in various public schools. Applied Scholastics is working to start a Hubbard program in public schools and plans to establish a campus to train educators in Hubbard's education methods. The Citizens Commission on Human Rights, whose members call themselves *psychbusters,* attacks its more orthodox competition in medicine and psychology.

As is common for such a group, defectors have formed their own sectarian splinter groups, following some of Hubbard's teachings but rejecting much of it as well. They tend to perceive the lower levels, the Dianetics part, as a good form of psychotherapy, but the higher levels, the Scientology theology, as pure science fiction. Some have become competitive, offering auditing at lower rates than those charged by Scientology. Others call themselves "Independent Scientologists," still accepting Scientology as their religion but rejecting the church organization.

Many teachings of Scientology are common to the New Age movement in general, and L. Ron Hubbard has influenced the popularization of many ideas common today in the movement. Some of Hubbard's ideas are so far out and the Church of Scientology so demanding and intolerant, however, that Scientology will probably never attract growing numbers of New Age people. On the other hand, if it becomes less radical, less intolerant, and more accepting of North American society, it may exist for a long time as a radical New Age wing.

Scientology and the Christian

Scientology and its emphasis on monism departs from Christian beliefs, as does the New Age movement in general. Although not entirely unique to Scientology, the belief in reincarnation contrasts to the scriptural teaching of resurrection.

Hubbard once said, "I know with certainty where I was and who I was in the last 80 trillion years." In teaching reincarnation, Hubbard knowingly drew on Eastern religion to such an extent that Scientology has been called "technological Buddhism." Scientologists acknowledge this relationship, claiming that "a Scientologist is first cousin to the Buddhist." An operating thetan in Scientology is much like a *bodhi* in Buddhism, an "enlightened one" who has been released from the "illusions" of the material world. One way to understand Scientology is as a rephrasing of reincarnation to fit modern, individualistic, self-improvement oriented North American culture.

Scientology is not unique in its belief in reincarnation. Many New Age groups today practice "past life regression" as a method to cure physical and psychological disorders. People on television shows now talk candidly about their past lives. Various polls have found that about one in four North Americans believe in reincarnation. This number rises to thirty percent among young people. Most surprising, this belief is almost as common among those who identify themselves as Christians as in the general population. The New Age version of reincarnation is a kind of positive thinking, onward and upward, evolutionary advance of the soul. It rejects or downplays the fatalism and the possibility of regressing in the next life to a lower animal form, typical of Eastern views of reincarnation.

In his book *Reincarnation vs. Resurrection*, John Snyder analyzes the doctrine of reincarnation. Following is a brief summary of his important points.

- Reincarnation opposes materialism. It affirms the importance of life's spiritual dimension and offers people hope for immortality and the possibility of reunion with loved ones. Because it does not require the admission of guilt or sin or the need to account to a personal god, it appeals to human pride and trust in one's own works and efforts.

- Retrocognition does not prove reincarnation. Although fraud and self-delusion explain many supposed cases of people's recall of a past life, others seem well documented. Yet a "memory" that goes back in time before one was born (retrocognition) does not prove that one actually lived a previous life. Various explanations for knowledge of the past have been offered. One explanation is demonic deception—spiritual forces working to deceive people into believing in reincarnation. Christians must seriously consider this possibility.

- Reincarnation is closely linked to the concept of karma. *Karma* means that an impersonal force in the universe sees that everyone gets what he or she deserves and that what happens to one in the next incarnation depends on what one does in this life. The problem is that, without ultimate standards of right or wrong, the individual must work out ideas of good and evil; salvation is entirely in one's own hands. History shows that people are incapable of saving themselves, so karma is a cruel condemnation of people for their sins.

- Reincarnation is centralized in monism. A soul can move from one person to another if everything is essentially one. The monist may talk about God, but believes that ultimately God and people and animals and nature are one. Monism does not accept a Creator God, and it disparages the creation as merely material, inferior to the spiritual. The Bible, in contrast, says both material and spiritual are part of creation and therefore worthy of redemption. While monism teaches that our ultimate goal is to be free of reincarnation and united with impersonal oneness, the Bible teaches our ultimate goal is to be free of sin and death in an eternal relationship with the Creator God.

- The Bible teaches resurrection, not reincarnation. Only three significant beliefs attempt to explain what happens after death: the materialist belief that we will cease to exist, the belief in reincarnation, and the Christian belief in resurrection and judgment. Believers in reincarnation often claim biblical support, but the Bible teaches that we die only once. The Christian can look forward to a new spiritual body, not reincarnation in yet another physical one or existence without a body. This view is based on the solid, empirical evidence of a historical case: the resurrection of Jesus Christ. After the resurrection, Jesus did not become pure spirit, but showed himself to his disciples in a transformed body that they still recognized. "The consummation of the new life awaits the new, resurrected body. This spiritual body is not a discorporate spirit but a true body, fitted for the age on a transformed earth."

As Christians examine Scientology, they should reflect on the warning of John in Revelation: "I warn everyone who hears the words of the prophecy of this book: If anyone adds anything to them, God will add to him the plagues described in this book.... He who testifies to these things says, 'Yes, I am coming soon'" (Rev. 22:18, 20).

Suggestions for Group Session

Getting Started

Try a word association exercise to get everyone involved in the discussion. (An overhead projector, chalkboard, or flip chart will be helpful.) What words come to mind when you hear the word *science?* What words do you think of when you hear the word *theology?* Do any of the words on either list describe *Scientology?*

Hubbard considered Dianetics a self-improvement technique but was quick to introduce Scientology as a religion. Why? Some say he was trying to protect himself from accusations and possible prosecution for practicing medicine without a license. Others say he wanted the protection of religious freedom and the reduction in taxes this status would grant. Regardless of Hubbard's motives, Scientology is now a "second-generation" religion with approximately one hundred thousand followers, at minimum estimates. What attracts these followers to what one critic calls "the most ruthless, the most classically terroristic, the most litigious and the most lucrative cult the country has every seen"?

Polls show that one in four North Americans (and almost one-third of young people) believe in reincarnation, a significant aspect of Scientology and New Age beliefs. Perhaps the most significant threat to Christianity from Scientology is the fact that these polls show "this belief is almost as common among those who identify themselves as Christians as in the general population." Why? Is reincarnation consistent with scriptural teachings? Can Christians accept a "piece" of Scientology?

Begin this session by reading together this litany based on 1 Corinthians 15:

> *These are the facts as we have received them,*
> *These are the truths that the Christian believes,*
> *This is the basis of all of our preaching:*
> *Christ died for sinners and rose from the tomb.*
> *These are the facts as we have received them:*
> *Christ has fulfilled what the Scriptures foretold,*
> *Adam's whole family in death had been sleeping,*
> *Christ through his rising restores us to life.*
> *These are the facts as we have received them:*

> *We shall be changed in the blink of an eye,*
> *Trumpets shall sound as we face life immortal;*
> *This is the victory through Jesus our Lord.*
>
> —"These Are the Facts As We Have Received Them," vv. 1, 2, 4
> Text: Michael Saward, 1971, © 1973, Hope Publishing Co., Carol Stream, IL 60188. All rights reserved. Used by permission.

If you wish to sing this litany, the music is found in *Psalter Hymnal*, 511. Alternate tunes are found in *Psalter Hymnal*, 12, 235; *Trinity Hymnal*, 300; *Presbyterian Hymnal*, 147, 360; *Rejoice in the Lord*, 414, 582.

Group Discussion and Activity

1. What common threads (such as similar early influences, beliefs, and practices) are appearing as we discuss each of these New Age leaders?

2. Read 1 Corinthians 15. (You may wish to ask one group member to read this passage from Eugene Peterson's *THE MESSAGE, The New Testament in Contemporary Language.*) Peterson interprets Paul's "if" in verse 19 in these words: "If all we get out of Christ is a little inspiration for a few short years, we're a pretty sorry lot." Try to imagine yourself in this situation. Do we sense Paul's fervor? His conviction that Christ *has* been raised?

3. Focus on 1 Corinthians 15:38-41. Verse 39 says, "All flesh is not the same: Men have one kind of flesh, animals have another, birds another and fish another." How do "these facts as we have received them" contrast with Hubbard's ideas of *thetans* who can occupy human, animal, and plant bodies over trillions of years?

4. Read 1 Corinthians 15:42-44 again. Does the New Age version of reincarnation as a "positive thinking, onward and upward, evolutionary advance of the soul" really offer people (even Christians) "some hope for a form of immortality and the possibility of being reunited with loved ones"? What's missing?

5. Peterson paraphrases 1 Corinthians 15:50 in these words: "I need to emphasize, friends, that our natural, earthly lives don't in themselves lead us by their very nature into the kingdom of God" (*THE MESSAGE*). How does the New Age emphasis on self-improvement and human potential training influence our culture? Where

might we be exposed to the idea that we can get "better and better"? Can we?

6. Reincarnation believers often quote such passages as Job 1:21; Jeremiah 1:4-5; Matthew 11:14 and 17:1-13; Luke 1:17; John 3:3-8 and 9:2-3; Galatians 1:15 and 6:7; and Hebrews 7:1-3. Look up several of these passages. Do any of them actually support reincarnation? (The *NIV Study Bible* or a Bible commentary might be helpful.)

7. Read Luke 20:35-36 and Hebrews 9:27-28. What comfort does the Christian have in knowing that we only die once?

Closing

Eugene Peterson challenges us with this contemporary translation of Paul's words in 1 Corinthians 15:33-34: "Think straight. Awaken to the holiness of life. No more playing fast and loose with resurrection facts. Ignorance of God is a luxury you can't afford in times like these" (*THE MESSAGE*).

Use these words from Heidelberg Catechism, A 57 as part of your closing prayer of thanksgiving for the comfort we have in the resurrection of the body: "Not only my soul will be taken immediately after this life to Christ its head, but even my very flesh, raised by the power of Christ, will be reunited with my soul, and made like Christ's glorious body."

"Amen. Come, Lord Jesus. The grace of the Lord Jesus be with God's people. Amen" (Rev. 22:20-21).

FOUR

HOLISTIC HEALTH PRACTICED BY NORMAN COUSINS

Cousins's Journey to New Age

Most of us have probably encountered Norman Cousins's beliefs in the seemingly innocent and scientifically proven supposition that laughter is good medicine. But entwined in Cousins's humor therapy and related techniques grouped under the umbrella of "holistic health" are his New Age beliefs.

Early Influences

Even as a little boy Norman Cousins tried to "discover exuberance." In 1922, at the age of ten, weak and underweight, he was sent to a tuberculosis sanitarium. Those six months in the sanitarium influenced his values and his personality. He discovered that the people in the sanitarium, both children and adults, tended to divide into two distinct groups: the optimists, who believed they would beat the odds and eventually recover and return to normal life, and the realists, who believed they were doomed to remain in the hospital until they died of tuberculosis. He was impressed that the optimistic group "had a far higher percentage of 'discharged as cured' outcomes than the kids in the other group. Even at the age of ten, I was being philosophically conditioned; I became aware of the power of the mind in overcoming disease."

Cousins went to New York City public schools and developed an interest in writing. During his years at Teacher's College at Columbia

University in New York, he studied with John Dewey and read about Gandhi for the first time. Deeply impressed, Cousins began to study Eastern thought. "The winds that blew from the East," he wrote, "helped to ventilate my thinking and to clear off the foggy negativism that was the fashion of the time."

In 1938, a friend gave him a copy of *Out of My Life and Thought* by Albert Schweitzer. Cousins saw a "magic junction" of Schweitzer's ideas with his own experience. He felt an immediate bond when he read Schweitzer's discussion of "the fellowship of those who bear the mark of pain." The life and thought of Schweitzer became a passionate interest that would last his entire life. Schweitzer admitted to Cousins that Buddhism greatly influenced his thinking, but he claimed that Jesus' teachings were not that different. Schweitzer said that Jesus did not claim to be the Messiah, but rather that he came to help people discover their natural goodness.

Career Paths

Cousins began his career in 1934 as educational editor of the *New York Evening Post*. The next year he moved on to book critic and then managing editor for *Current History*. In 1940 he became executive editor of the *Saturday Review of Literature*, and in 1942, at only thirty years of age, managing editor and president.

Given complete freedom to run the magazine as he saw fit, he shortened the title to *Saturday Review* and broadened the coverage from literary reviews to include current events, education, travel, and social issues. He "exemplified the liberal democratic spirit of the Roosevelt era" and wrote influential editorials on topics such as world peace, environmental problems, the United Nations, and violence in the media. In later years he said, "nothing in my life, next to my family [his wife and five daughters], has meant more to me than the *Saturday Review.*"

In 1945, twelve days after the first atomic bomb was dropped, Cousins published "Modern Man Is Obsolete," an editorial that argued that in the new atomic age we must develop a world federation and regard ourselves as world citizens. National sovereignty has become an "obstruction in the circulatory system of the world," he wrote. Throughout the fifties and sixties, he worked diligently for world peace, lecturing in India, Pakistan, Ceylon, and Japan; writing; and organizing cultural exchanges with the Soviet Union. Cousins became an independent but effective international negotiator, discussing peace initiatives with presidents and prime ministers, including Nikita Khrushchev. In 1971 he was awarded the United Nations Peace Medal.

Cousins criticized our system of education for teaching people to be "tribe-conscious" and focusing too much on people's differences. He also believed that our educational system should abandon the outmoded division between East and West in the areas of religion and philosophy, accepting the New Age idea that all religions are alike in their fundamental teachings. These teachings could form the basis for peace and world unity.

He criticized Christianity for having "become strangely adjacent to the crisis of man," content with individual moral and spiritual matters when it should be a dominant force in bringing about unity. Cousins completely overlooked the gospel message; he thought that Christianity, which he once referred to as "the greatest idea ever to be taken up by the mind of man," was a vision of how to achieve the "brotherhood of man."

Health Problems

In 1954, at the age of thirty-nine, Cousins was diagnosed with a serious coronary occlusion and advised to stay in bed for a few months. He ignored this advice and continued his usual round of activities, including work and sports. Three years later he met the famous heart specialist, Paul Dudley White, who told him he had done the right thing. "The meeting with White," he said later, "was something of a landmark in my life. It gave me confidence in my rapport with my own body. It reinforced my conviction that the human mind can discipline the body, can set goals for itself, can somehow comprehend its own potentiality and move resolutely forward."

In 1964, at the age of forty-nine, Cousins contracted ankylosing spondylitis, a deterioration of connective tissues that resulted in severe and painful inflammation of the spine and joints. He found it increasingly difficult to move his jaw, neck, arms, hands, and legs. According to his own report, his doctors gave him only one chance in five hundred of recovery. He set out to prove them wrong based on his "fast-growing conviction that a hospital is no place for a person who is seriously ill." He decried its "surprising lack of respect for basic sanitation"; the extensive use of X rays, tranquilizers, and painkillers; things being run more for the staff's convenience than that of the patients; and the poorly balanced diet of processed foods containing preservatives and dyes. "I became convinced that nothing a hospital could provide in the way of technological marvels was as helpful as an atmosphere of compassion."

Reflecting on what he had learned in years of reporting on medical issues and especially from his own childhood illness, Cousins decided not to accept his fate passively. When he was told that one of the many possible causes of his disease was a malfunctioning endocrine system, he recalled reading that it could be caused by the influence of negative emotions on body chemistry. He asked himself, "If negative emotions produce negative chemical changes in the body, wouldn't the positive emotions produce positive chemical changes? Is it possible that love, hope, faith, laughter, confidence, and the will to live have therapeutic value? Do chemical changes occur only on the downside?"

Cousins suspected that his painkillers might be hindering his recovery but wondered how to handle the intense pain without them. He conceived the idea of using humor to relieve his pain. He watched old television comedies, and people read to him from books such as *The Treasury of American Humor* and *The Enjoyment of Laughter*. He discovered that ten minutes of laughing relieved his pain to such an extent to allow him a few hours of sleep. This began his nearly full recovery. He concluded that "the will to live is not a theoretical abstraction, but a physiologic reality with therapeutic characteristics," and hypothesized that laughter may have caused his brain to release endorphins, which act as painkillers.

Although by this time Cousins was famous in literary circles and among peace activists, his "miraculous" recovery led to his greatest fame. An article in the *New England Journal of Medicine* first described it, and his best-selling book, *Anatomy of an Illness as Perceived by the Patient*, published in 1979, later detailed it. The article in the NEJM produced three thousand letters from doctors, both critical and supportive, and many invitations to speak to faculty and students at medical centers around the country. Cousins's philosophy about holistic health spread as he not only accepted but significantly contributed to the New Age idea that much illness is self-imposed.

A New Age Leader

Many have tested and accepted Cousins's idea that laughter can aid in recovery—an idea now classified as "humor therapy." Laughter is now believed to reduce stress, provide a new perspective on society, help confront personal problems, and increase creativity and flexibility. A recent report on the research of Dr. Lee Berk concluded that "people who laugh frequently decrease their stress hormones and increase the body's defenses against disease." Echoing Cousins, Berk claims that laughter "helps the body go back to a normal state. People should go out of their way to be mirthful." And like Cousins, he quotes Proverbs 17:22: "A cheerful heart is good medicine." Many reports indicate hospitals and nursing homes are introducing "humor rooms" and "laughter wagons" as part of their treatment programs. Some psychologists now offer workshops and retreats to teach those in high stress jobs to "lighten up" and laugh.

Most Christians, even in the medical field, might concur wholeheartedly with Cousins but for his New Age beliefs that have influenced the holistic health movement. People, he believed, are "naturally good" but imperfect. They have a "propensity for error" (*evil* is not part of his vocabulary), but their innate creative potential, the evolutionary development of humanity, can balance this. "God," declared Cousins, is "the Ultimate Force that prevents the cosmic void from becoming absolute." At one point he speaks of the "divine cosmos." He said the "basic law of life" is that the universe is gradually emerging from chaos to greater and greater integration, and we should devote our lives to contributing to this move toward oneness. "There is no more awesome evidence of a Deity than that which exists in human potentiality." He thought it logical that we are the result of a "Great Design," but he rejected the idea of a Creator God in favor of a monistic "ultimate force" holding everything together.

After Cousins retired from the *Saturday Review,* he became a full-time advocate of holistic health. Besides teaching and researching in the Department of Psychiatry and Biobehavioral Science at the UCLA School of Medicine, he counseled seriously ill patients as their "responsible cheerleader." In his writing during this period, notably *Human Options* (1981) and *Head First: The Biology of Hope and the Healing Power of the Human Spirit* (1989), he explained the medical research that has led to the development of a new branch of medicine. Psychoneuroimmunology deals with the interaction among the brain, the immune system, and the endocrine system. Excerpts of *Head First* were published in several leading magazines, and *Reader's Digest* printed a condensed version. The mind-body relationship and its healing potential have since been discussed by many others, most notably in the popular books of Dr. Bernie Siegel and Dr. Deepak Chopra.

In the sixties, Cousins became a friend of Bill Moyers, then a White House assistant. Many years later Moyers went to California to interview him, and Cousins argued that Moyers should produce a television series about the growing field of mind-body medicine. After Cousins's death, the popular series *Healing and the Mind* was broadcast on PBS and published in book form. It topped the best-seller list in 1993 and is now available on videocassette.

Probably almost every American has been exposed to Norman Cousins's beliefs and practices by way of his prolific writing, his role in world affairs, and his influential positions in the fields of journalism and medicine. Christians, especially within the health care profession, must, in the light of Scripture, separate what is sound in the holistic health movement from what is New Age. We will attempt some of that sorting in the second part of this chapter.

What Is *Holistic Health*?

Holistic health is difficult to describe, because it includes a diverse collection of practices, theories, and beliefs. First of all, not all holistic health is New Age. Some reasonable arguments for a holistic approach to health have nothing to do with New Age thought or practices. Most physicians today are holistic in the sense that they believe patients need adequate exercise, a proper diet, skills for stress management, and a positive mental outlook.

A "Mode of Spirituality"

Nevertheless, much of what is under the rubric of holistic health is New Age and, conversely, holistic health (some now prefer the term *behavioral medicine*) is a central concern of the New Age movement. Russell Chandler in *Understanding the New Age* says that many people first encounter New Age ideas when they go to a holistic practitioner, who may describe the human body as a "complex energetic interference pattern interpenetrated by the organized bioenergetic field of the etheric body." Some have contended that the entire New Age movement can be seen as a new healing movement in Western culture.

Holistic practitioners differ somewhat in their view of conventional medicine, which they refer to as *allopathic medicine*. They typically argue for "eclectic pragmatism," which permits practitioners to use whatever combination works best, favoring what conventional society thinks of as the mystical and the occult. They criticize conventional medicine's focus on surgery and drugs but recognize the need for such interventions in crisis situations. Few would recommend an alternative therapy for appendicitis or a serious infection, but they would supplement conventional treatment with an alternative therapy that, they believe, would greatly aid the healing process. They argue that traditional methods rely too heavily on allopathic medicine. Surgery or drugs might be unnecessary with the precaution of preventive alternative techniques. Holistic health practitioners want to shift Western culture's thinking about health so that traditional techniques become less necessary.

The Association for Holistic Health distinguishes holistic health as "person oriented rather than disease oriented." Traditional medicine treats symptoms rather than the whole person. Each person is a unique interplay of body, mind, emotion, and spirit; because physical and nonphysical spheres interpenetrate in a complex causal system, health and healing depend on an understanding of the whole person.

Holistic health has been called a "mode of spirituality." Chandler says, "As New Agers ask the age-old question of spiritual transformation, 'What must I (or the world) do to be saved?' it emerges as, 'What must I—and the planet—do to be healed?'" Often the answer is found in Eastern religious or Western occult traditions, which suggest that we have ultimate control over our own health and well-being.

Some in the movement connect holistic health and the feminist movement; they identify allopathic medicine as male and holistic medicine as female. The holistic health movement attempts to restore a lost balance between the male and female principles in the universe. Some also believe that healing for women is different than it is for men and therefore requires different practices.

New Age healing includes belief in evolution. As humanity evolves toward a higher form we should expect general improvements in health and longevity, particularly at this time when, as New Agers believe, we are at the point of a major evolution.

Paul Reisser says, "Holistic health is, in essence, the banner under which the [New Age] is making its move into the realm of health and medicine. . . .[It] does not appear nearly as concerned with changing the way medicine is practiced as it is with changing the fundamental orientation of people toward themselves, the universe, and especially the supernatural realm" (*New Age Medicine*).

A Variety of Techniques and Beliefs

Some have said that holistic health is largely an outgrowth of the turn East, while others emphasize beliefs already present in the West. Advertisements in any New Age magazine reveal a startling variety of healing practices from around the world, particularly those found in China or India or among Native Americans. All proponents agree that healing is ultimately a mysterious process, that no one technique can make exclusive claims, and that everything must be individualized to be effective. One commentator says, "Most are more interested in defending their world view than the particular technique they use."

Following is a sample of some of the most discussed therapies, beginning with those most acceptable to traditional medicine and moving toward the occult fringe.

Biofeedback: Controlling involuntary processes in the body such as brain waves, heart rate, blood pressure, muscle tension, and temperature by mentally "feeding back" to the body information gained from various measurement instruments, thus gaining control of a body function generally considered beyond conscious control. Although reports are mixed, biofeedback seems useful in some situations, especially for relaxing muscles to prevent or cure headaches caused by muscle contractions. Biofeedback is an accepted technique in some hospitals and is covered by some insurance companies.

Guided Imagery (or visualization): "The use of positive, affirming mental pictures to obtain goals. A vivid mental picture of a desired goal is held in the mind as though it already were accomplished." This technique, introduced in the seventies to help athletes and musicians perform better, is now widely used in these fields. Alternative health practice and some medical doctors promote it to combat infections, cancer, and pain, and to aid in recovery after surgery. Many consider visualization an entirely natural process, but others believe that they are accessing their "superconscious" or "Buddha nature" or "god within."

Acupuncture: "Needles are inserted under the skin at various points to treat various conditions by manipulating *ch'i* [also spelled *qi*], the universal life force, which flows through the body along energy pathways called meridians." It is based on the ancient Chinese theory that hundreds of points on the body can be identified and stimulated to cure illness and reduce pain by restoring a proper flow of *ch'i* and balancing the *yin* and *yang* forces in the body. Major medical centers for the control of chronic pain now use acupuncture, often without reference to the underlying Taoist theory. Acupuncture's effectiveness is the subject of considerable disagreement.

Chiropractic: "The manipulation of the spine and joints by hand to rebalance or repair the body's neurological functions and restore the body's energies." Robert Fuller, in *Alternative Medicine and American Religious Life*, traces the origins of chiropractic to Franz Mesmer's nineteenth century "therapeutic hypnosis." In addition to influencing the beginnings of Christian Science, New Thought, and other such religious groups, "mesmerism" was at the root of both chiropractic and osteopathic medicine. Rejected by the American Medical Association, each became established as an alternative healing system. D. D. Palmer established chiropractic on the principle that, as Mesmer had said, all illnesses have one cause—the disruption of the flow in the "divine force" in the body by "deranged nerves." This idea of a "divine force," Fuller explains, was gradually lost over the years, and most people came to consider chiropractic (as well as osteopathy) a totally natural process. In recent years, New Age healers have begun to use chiropractic and reintroduce the metaphysical dimension, arguing once more that it works by a flow of a supernatural power.

Therapeutic Touch (TT): "Energy transfer therapy developed by Dora van Gelder Kunz, a clairvoyant and meditation teacher, and Dolores Krieger, a nurse. The universal life force is transmitted [from the person playing the role of the healer] through touch, holding the hands over the affected area of the body, or brushing the patient's energy field with strokes of the hand." The individual must be "inwardly receptive" to healing, but energy can flow even without contact because of a "human field which extends beyond the discernible mass which we perceive as man." Therapeutic touch is said to reduce pain, tension, and anxiety; increase hemoglobin levels; and detect tumors by sensing areas that are too hot or cold. Detractors call it a form of "New Age mumbo jumbo." They charge it to be "paranormal and religious activity masquerading as science," without a legitimate place in medicine. One critic says, "I see therapeutic touch as a form of faith healing that has captured the imagination of a few nurses [tens of thousands, according to a *Time* magazine report] who happen to be in pretty powerful positions of influence within the nursing profession."

Homeopathy: Treating a disease by "using extremely small, nontoxic doses of plant, mineral, animal, or chemical substances which in overdose would have a similar effect of causing such a disease in a well person." Samuel Hahneman, a German doctor, began this system of treatment in 1810. He claimed that illness is not so much a material condition as a "derangement in the life force in man." Traditional medicine is criticized for treating a human as "exclusively a physio-electrochemical organism." Homeopathy, by contrast, is said to be able to "attune, correct, and purify the human organism so that it functions with efficiency and sensitivity." Excluded from the American Medical Association and from public funding for medical schools, homeopathy fell into disrepute and obscurity, but with the support of New Agers it is making a comeback. Theoretically, it should cure any symptom, but homeopathy is used mostly to treat coughs, colds, aches and pains, allergies, and other "ill-defined complaints." According to *Healthier Times* magazine, homeopathy is a "proven alternative to orthodox medical care," and "a high percentage of children's ailments respond particularly well to homeopathy." Opponents call it a "shotgun approach" to treatment.

Herbology: The treatment of specific symptoms or the attempt to improve one's general health with herbs. Herbs are advertised as useful as "body cleaners, rejuvenators, tonics, and relaxers." Herbal catalogues offer explanations on how to use alfalfa leaf, bayberry bark, bee pollen [the "miracle food"], bugleweed, Canada snake root, chickweed, dandelion, eucalyptus, hawthorn, mandrake, mugwort, skunk cabbage root, myrrh, sage, and many others. Herbs are advertised for treating arthritis, cataracts, PMS, asthma, bronchitis, and kidney disorders, headaches, backaches, indigestion, loss of appetite, insomnia, weight and memory loss, colic, and every other imaginable ailment. One enthusiast says, "Fortunately, the self-help and holistic health movements of the past few years have rekindled interest in the gentler, more natural healing methods. Herbs as alternative medicine are once again becoming popular in America." Unfortunately, discerning the efficacy of the multitude of herbs is difficult. New Agers are studying with herbalists and shamans all over the world, returning to start schools and mail-order courses in "planetary herbology."

Ayurveda: A traditional form of healing in India; meaning "knowledge of life." Ayurveda is said to "hold mind and body as one and the same, and disease is the culminating manifestation of a life that has lost its balance." Claiming to have developed a synthesis of Ayurveda with Western medicine and quantum physics, Deepak Chopra has become a powerful force in New Age medicine. His method is to help his patients communicate with their innermost being—the eternal spirit that pervades the body—using music, touch, smell, massage, and diet. In his best-seller *Ageless Body, Timeless Mind,* Chopra argues that our bodies learn to age and that aging can be unlearned. In a June 24, 1996, article entitled "Faith and Healing," *Time* magazine called Chopra the "emperor of the soul." The July 1996 issue of *Youthworker Update* lists Demi Moore, Michael Jackson, Winona Ryder, Olivia Newton-John, Naomi Judd, and former Beatle George Harrison among Chopra fans and notes that it's an Oprah Winfrey interview and his embracement by "Hollywood glitterati that demonstrates he's made it into the holy high-rollers club."

These eight practices represent some of the holistic health therapies that have influenced traditional medical practices. Some are now established as alternative healing systems; some border on the occult fringe.

From a New Age Perspective

Although all holistic health is not New Age, certain aspects of the holistic health movement clearly are. We'll examine five New Age perspectives relative to holistic health.

- **Healing comes from within.**

    According to New Agers, we are each responsible for our own health. Marilyn Fergusen in her book *The Aquarian Conspiracy* claims that "the healer inside us is the wisest, most complex, integrated entity in the universe." Bernie Siegel's *Love, Medicine, and Miracles* tells patients that "the body heals, not the therapy. . . . The body can utilize any form of energy for healing as long as the patient believes in it. Let's say I recommended eating three peanut butter sandwiches a day to cure cancer. Some people would get well and claim it was the peanut butter that did it. Then even more people would have hope, eat peanut butter, and get better, too. But we know it's not the peanut butter. It's their hope and the changes they produce in their lives while they're on the new therapy." Positive attitude is Siegel's most important factor in health and healing. Any form of medical treatment is only a way to "buy time during which I can help the patient find the will to live, change, and heal." Belief in God, vitamins, and hypnotherapy are all equally acceptable to him. The role of the doctor or other healer is to help us get rid of anything that stands in the way of the body's innate ability to heal itself.

- **A person is composed of three interrelated parts: body, mind, and spirit.**
  In the New Age view, health comes from a strong integration of body, mind, and spirit. Their notion of this is often confusing and ambiguous. The claim that "body is mind, and mind is spirit" does not help; nor does Chopra's argument that "your mind is not in your brain, but in every cell of your body. One cell speaks to another." Clearly all this reinforces monism, but we are left with questions about the difference among the three and their relationship. We can probably agree that our modern society has created an unhealthy division between body, mind, and spirit. Medicine has focused on the body, psychology on the mind, and religion on the spirit, each staying out of the others' territory, thus loosing the ancient understanding of a vital link. New Agers believe this division has blinded many to the value of the emerging holistic approach.

- **A universal energy flows from the universe into the individual.**
  Almost all New Age people accept Cousins's belief in what he calls a "life force." New Agers believe in a spiritual energy found throughout the body that unites us with each other and with the universe (or God, or the "great All"). With Fritjof Capra's claim that the universe is made of energy patterns rather than matter, New Age literature uses energy to explain almost everything. Even the biblical references to the *Logos* or the Holy Spirit are equated with this "life force." Although the term "universal energy" does not sound foreign, New Age literature today clearly emphasizes the Eastern sources of this idea.

  New Agers believe that what we experience as disease or pain is caused by a disturbance in our energy flow. The solution is to restore balance, using whichever one or combination of available techniques works best for us. A healer is essentially anyone who can help us do this. On the one hand, New Agers argue that we all have access to this energy, but on the other hand, many healers build their reputations on claims of having an innate or learned special command of this power. Most, but not all, holistic health advocates believe in this energy. Most of the theory behind the various practices refer to it. This idea of contact with a spiritual power source, more than anything else, attracts many to holistic health.

No one has ever shown empirically that universal energy exists or can be drawn upon at will. One critic calls this "a mystical concept extracted from a distant corner of Eastern philosophy, sanitized in Western scientific trappings, taught to well-intentioned members of helping professions who are looking for new ways to relieve suffering." An impersonal, supernatural force convinces such people that they are in contact with a higher power, but they are still in control. They do not have to submit to the will of an all-powerful God. Invisible energy may seem innocuous or silly to some of us, according to another critic, but the results of practices involving such belief may be exposure to spiritual forces instead of God. One commentator stated that "rituals, yoga, meditation, massage, special diets, the use of crystals, gemstones, plants, and colors are all ways to generate greater consciousness of this healing power and to activate it in the suffering person." Dr. Larry Dossey's recent popular book, *Healing Words*, argues that prayer aids healing because it appeals to the "nonlocal aspect of the psyche, the part of us that is infinite in space and time and is Divine."

- **Personal and universal wholeness is more important than a cure.**
New Age thinking distinguishes between being cured and achieving wholeness. To achieve wholeness, one needs to "correct the underlying disharmony causing the problem," which demands healing that transcends the physical body into the spiritual dimension. Spirituality is a constant, yet elusive, element in New Age healing. One healer says, "By cultivating our spiritual aspect, we can change mental and emotional patterns from within, thereby establishing attitudes and beliefs that lead to life-long health and well-being." Generally, New Agers do not advocate any particular spirituality; they urge us to find whatever inspires us. They also suggest that wholeness as an isolated individual is impossible. Philosopher Renee Wever says that holistic health proposes that the "primary cause of disease is a disconnectedness from the flow and rhythm of the whole" both within the individual and within groups of individuals. "Health is the automatic reward of living in accordance with the cosmic order."

- **Traditional Western medicine is useful but inadequate.**
  To New Agers, holistic health is but one part, although a very important part, of an evolution toward a new way of thinking that is absent from conventional medicine. Although New Agers value Western medicine, particularly its use of modern technology in a crisis situation, they criticize it as focused only on the immediate physical manifestation of illness rather than on the responsible holistic social and spiritual context. Fritjof Capra says that "although medicine has contributed to the elimination of certain diseases, it has not necessarily restored health." New Agers are wary of prescription drugs, expensive medical treatments, and the unfair monopoly in health care while defending their own emphasis on the experimental approach to truth. The rigorous standards of Western culture cannot test New Agers' "natural" explanations of illness and health. New Agers' interest in ancient philosophies and religions carries over into medicine; they feel this dimension is of little concern to Western medical practitioners.

  The New Age view is separate from both conventional medicine and Christianity. They accuse conventional medical practice of materialism—accepting only that which can be demonstrated in controlled experiments and rejecting the supernatural's influence in the healing process. The Christian perspective is too self-effacing, seeing God as a person and petitioning him for healing.

Holistic Health and the Christian

How much of holistic health can the Christian accept? First of all, we must remind ourselves that not all holistic health practitioners preach New Age concepts. Biofeedback seems innocuous when separated from the New Age theory. The use of hypnosis or visualization in curing does not seem inherently wrong either. The emphasis in holistic health on preventive medicine is good; no one can deny that the specialization and heavy patient loads in modern medicine have generated problems. A personalized approach that emphasizes a healthy lifestyle presents obvious advantages.

We can also agree with the New Age practitioner that people have a spiritual dimension that can be important in some healing processes, that wellness or wholeness is more than physical, that people should acknowledge their own responsibility for their health and not trust entirely in drugs and surgery. Christian doctors have always recognized this, and they share with New Age healers the goal of making the patient well in a broader, more holistic sense than only bodily healing.

The New Age view of holistic health contains some pitfalls, however. Christians run the danger of falling prey to these snares:

- accepting views or practices not proven to have any scientific value
- ignoring conventional medicine that could be of more help
- developing a sense of guilt if healing doesn't occur
- believing in an impersonal universal energy one can control at will
- getting involved with the occult
- beginning with a seemingly innocent program of exercises or diet, but eventually accepting a related belief system antithetical to Christianity
- thinking one can be whole and healthy apart from a personal relationship with Jesus Christ

The Christian agrees that wholeness is more than physical health but has a different definition of wholeness and how to achieve it. Although supernatural powers are at work in the world, they are not impersonal and amenable to our control. Both Old and New Testaments specifically prohibit us from approaching such dangerous and deceptive powers. Supernatural healing cannot be real if not from God.

Also, because of the fall, the human body succumbs to flaws and deterioration that no amount of positive thinking can overcome. New Agers sometimes speak of death as a healing event, rather than a failure to heal. This conflicts with the Christian view that death is the great enemy, which only Christ has the power to conquer. Paul tells us to accept our state in life, including physical affliction. God has the power to heal, but we must also be willing to accept illness and death without granting it ultimate importance in our lives. Physical and mental health are pointless apart from a healthy relationship with God.

Christians trust that prayer may heal disease. New Agers agree, but they have a different explanation for why it works. While a New Ager sees "miraculous" cure as the consequence of tapping into a healing power, the Christian believes that God miraculously intervenes in natural processes.

Jesus is Lord of all, including illness and death, and only faith in him brings wholeness. "For you who revere my name, the sun of righteousness will rise with healing in its wings" (Mal. 4:2). The *Prayer Book of 1662* says, "Shew us the light of thy countenance, and we shall be whole." Ultimately the health and wholeness of the individual human body, as well as that of the entire creation, will be restored in the great day of the Lord.

Suggestions for Group Session

Getting Started

Often good health ranks at the top of the list of things people value most. Perhaps we think of health as a sense of well-being or the lack of disease. Sometimes we do not think of it at all until we lose it. Given health's elusive nature and the value we give it, it's no surprise that the holistic health movement has had such a tremendous impact on our society in the last few decades.

Christians face two challenges in regard to the holistic health movement. First, since the holistic health movement includes a diverse collection of practices, theories, and beliefs, defining it is difficult. Second, since not all holistic health is New Age, we must determine what is acceptable in the light of God's Word.

Some of the beliefs and leadership roles of six New Agers in this book may be unrelated to our everyday activities. Given Norman Cousins's important influence, however, almost all have been exposed to his holistic health practices and New Age beliefs—likely in ways that we would have difficulty identifying. This aspect of New Age has definitely "shifted out of the counterculture into the mainstream of society" (Groothuis, *Unmasking the New Age*).

The following discussion questions and activities are designed to help your group define holistic health and develop some guidelines for responding to the movement. By increasing our awareness of the benefits and dangers of holistic health beliefs and practices, we can make sound lifestyle and health-care decisions consistent with our faith in our Creator God and faithful Father.

Begin this session with a prayer to thank God for his faithfulness and providential care and to ask God for strength and grace to trust him even when our health fails.

Group Discussion and Activity

1. Read Luke 4:38-41; 5:12-14; 7:1-9. These and other passages in the gospels describe Jesus' miraculous healing ministry. Imagine yourself as Luke, the physician, well educated in the best schools of the day. What might you think of Jesus rebuking the fever in Peter's mother-in-law, laying his hands on those with various illnesses, touching the leper, commending the faith of the centurion? Would you doubt the professional credibility of this carpenter from Nazareth?

2. Have you experienced Cousins's conviction "that a hospital is no place for a person who is seriously ill"? What factors might contribute to this rather negative evaluation? What changes would you like to see? Consider the supportive care offered by hospice programs to encourage patients to continue relationships and familiar routines. What, if any, of the hospice philosophy could enhance a hospital stay?

3. Do you agree that "laughter is the best medicine" or, as Proverbs 17:22 says, "A cheerful heart is good medicine"? What effect does someone's sense of humor have on you, especially if you're sick or "down in the dumps"? Are some of us naturally more cheerful (or melancholic) than others?

4. Some in the New Age movement go so far as to say that we initiate illness so that we can learn from it (an idea based on their belief that we can control a universal energy flow or "life force"). Why would anyone *want* to be ill? What lessons can we learn from illness?

5. Ecclesiastes 7:3 says, "Sorrow is better than laughter, because a sad face is good for the heart." Does this passage contradict Proverbs 17:22? The note for Ecclesiastes 7:1 in the *NIV Study Bible* explains that "happy times generally teach us less than hard times." Could our fear of these hard times (specifically illness) increase our interest in holistic health practices and decrease our desire to discern what is good from what is probably just a "quick fix"? What prompts people to seek a cure at all costs?

6. Of the five New Age perspectives relative to holistic health discussed in this chapter (pages 70-73), which one (or more) do you find the easiest to identify as anti-Christian in your own environment (in literature, in the media, in medical services, and in other contacts with the holistic health movement)? Where have you encountered these beliefs?

7. This chapter identified seven dangers for the Christian (page 74). Which of these dangers particularly concern you personally? Other members of your family? Those you serve, especially if you are involved in health care, education, or ministry? (You may want to break into smaller groups to discuss these questions.)

8. Without being alarmists, what is the role of the church in equipping its members to sort out what is acceptable about the holistic health movement? What can your local congregation do?

Closing

Read Matthew 9:1-7. Jesus explained to the teachers of the law (and to us) why he healed the sick: "so that you may know that the Son of Man has authority on earth to forgive sins. . . ." (v. 6). Ultimately only our spiritual sickness will separate us from our Savior. Thank God that "by his wounds we are healed" (Isa. 53:5).

Close this session by reading this prayer in unison or by singing this hymn from *Psalter Hymnal,* 363; *The Worshipping Church,* 409; or *The Hymnbook* (1955), 179.

> *O be our mighty healer still, O Lord of life and death;*
> *Restore and strengthen, soothe and bless with your almighty breath.*
> *On hands that work and eyes that see, your healing wisdom pour,*
> *That whole and sick and weak and strong may praise you evermore.*
>
> —"Thine Arm, O Lord, in Days of Old," stanza 3
> Text: Edward H. Plumptre, 1866, alt.

FIVE

THE PSYCHIC LIFE CELEBRATED BY SHIRLEY MACLAINE

MacLaine's Journey to New Age

Shirley MacLaine—one of Hollywood's best known actresses, nightclub performer, world traveler, best-seller author—is seldom content with what many would consider outstanding success. Always "in search of herself," she has become a "celebrity evangelist for the New Age." Both her "critics and fans alike concur that MacLaine has done more than any other single person in recent times to soften the ground for people to believe and participate in things they once avoided for fear of being thought 'flaky.'"

Early Influences

Shirley MacLaine grew up in a well-educated and talented family, which included her brother, actor Warren Beatty. She later said, however, "My parents never fulfilled their creative potential. I grew up surrounded by anxiety and disappointment."

Sent to ballet school at the age of three to strengthen her ankles, Shirley devoted herself to dancing and continued lessons throughout her childhood. Disappointment struck when, at the age of sixteen, she was told she had grown too tall for serious ballet roles. Someone suggested she try musical comedy. Her first experience was in a touring summer company of *Oklahoma*. At the end of the summer she was offered a job in the London production of *Oklahoma*, but her father convinced her to first finish high school. Two years later, in 1952, she was in New York dancing in the chorus line of *Me and Juliet*.

As an understudy in the musical *Pajama Game*, she got her big break. One night when she replaced an injured star, a Hollywood producer saw her and signed her to a film-acting contract. Her brother later said, "Realization seemed to come to her in that show that *she* was more interesting than her techniques as a dancer, about which she had always had a lot of anxieties."

When she arrived in Los Angeles, young, impressionable, and with only a high school education, MacLaine quickly became absorbed in the glitter of the Hollywood film industry. Always restless and inquisitive, she joined the so-called Rat Pack, which included Frank Sinatra, Dean Martin, and Sammy Davis, Jr. She admits that she sometimes accepted roles in less than outstanding films in order to work with these friends.

In 1954, at the age of twenty, MacLaine married actor Steve Parker. "I felt I needed protection, some grounding," she said later. They moved to Los Angeles to begin her movie career, but the marriage was soon in trouble. "Shirley had this drive," explained Parker, "this push . . . she didn't want to be surrounded by a white picket fence." Their daughter, Stephanie Sachiko, was born in 1956, but Shirley admits she "never really embraced the role of motherhood." Although she and Parker did not divorce until 1982, they agreed that each of them was free to have other relationships.

In the seventies, she became sexually promiscuous. She believed this lifestyle liberated women from the old double standard, but she soon decided such relationships did not offer enough communication. Also in the seventies, she involved herself in the civil rights movement and protested the Viet Nam War.

In 1972, after the U.S. restored diplomatic relations with China, that country invited her to lead a delegation of women on a visit. On her return, she publicly admired the communist revolution and set about writing, directing, and producing a film, *The Other Half of the Sky: A China Memoir*, for which she received a nomination for best documentary in 1975.

Some thought she would leave acting entirely and devote herself to politics, but, always restless, she soon turned to something new. She began to spend time at a place near her California home called the *Ashram*, where, for $1,300 a week, she participated in yoga exercises, jogging, calisthenics, and weightlifting. She later stated that the Ashram was a catalyst in leading her to believe in "karmic consciousness" and "the metaphysical dimension."

Her first book, published in 1970, became a best-seller. *Don't Fall Off the Mountain* discussed her career in films, her travels, and the beginnings of her interest in the mystical. She reports that although her parents were not church-going people, they sent her to a Baptist Sunday School; nevertheless, by adulthood she considered herself an atheist. Her circle of friends largely consisted of actors, writers, and politicians, most of whom were unbelievers in anything supernatural. She became, she said, one of those "what I see, I believe type of people." Yet she soon found that, as with many New Agers who reject Christianity, atheism did not satisfy her—something was missing from her life. A Christian might say that her soul was restless for God, but she defined her problem as a "loneliness for myself."

She traveled extensively. "I would make a beeline out of the country in an effort to find myself," she explained later. Rather than the beaches, ski resorts, and other haunts of the rich and famous, MacLaine visited such places as the mountains of Bhutan and the Masai tribe in Africa. In a country where young people commonly speak of "finding myself," MacLaine became the ultimate searcher for self. Her career took second place to this quest. "I was most interested in working out my own identity, and characters I played took away from that."

Traveling introduced her to new ideas. Indian culture felt so familiar to her that she became convinced she had been there in a previous life, although at that time she claims she knew nothing about the idea of reincarnation. Also, she said, "Things in my life were happening too coincidentally to be coincidental. I began to see there are no accidents." The purpose of life, she concluded, is "to purify the soul and understand we are basically good, we are basically divine, we are basically God."

Career Paths

MacLaine's first Hollywood role was in an Alfred Hitchcock film, *The Trouble with Harry* (1955), which "established her as an unconventional presence in American cinema. Her redheaded good looks, impish humor, natural timing and air of vulnerability made her popular as a kook or a kindly floozie." In the late sixties she tired of light comedic roles and turned to more serious drama. By 1970, with several Academy Award nominations, she was one of Hollywood's best known actresses. She also began to write books and perform in a nightclub act as a singer and dancer.

Her second book, *You Can't Get There from Here*, published in 1975, discussed her work in political campaigns and the China tour. This book bore much criticism as being naive and unrealistic about communist China's many problems. It did not sell as well as the first, and by 1977 MacLaine was back on the Hollywood scene with another nomination for best actress for her role in *The Turning Point*.

The driven MacLaine continued her acting and writing roles. According to a feature article in *Time* magazine, on her forty-ninth birthday in 1983 MacLaine "projected" what she wanted to accomplish in the next year: an Oscar for her role in *Terms of Endearment*, the best-seller list for *Out on a Limb*, and a successful act on Broadway. *Time* called this "an almost greedy welter of ambitions," but amazingly, she achieved all of them. In accepting her Oscar, she said, "God bless the potential we all have for making anything possible if we think we deserve it. I deserve this!"

Although still an accomplished singer, dancer, and actress, MacLaine has decided that her books are most important in her life. "I couldn't give up writing," she says. "Performing belongs to everyone, writing belongs just to me." She's convinced that her view of life is spreading rapidly through North American society and supports this with the fact that she's no longer treated as a "kook." Shirley MacLaine jokes that poke fun of her beliefs are evidence that people are now comfortable with the New Age view. "Once you joke about something, you know that it's settled into the culture."

A New Age Leader

True to MacLaine's projections, *Out on a Limb*, a personal account of her increasing if not enthusiastic acceptance of New Age teachings, has sold over three million copies since 1983. Full of New Age characters and New Age language, it has introduced thousands of people to New Age and occult ideas. Her close friends tried to persuade her not to reveal all of this so publicly; they feared she would be ridiculed and her career destroyed. Proceeding with publication, then, took considerable courage. Indeed, MacLaine jokes began as soon as the book was published and continue to this day.

Yet, far from ending her career, *Out on a Limb* seems only to have added new dimensions and helped propel her superstar status. Thousands of people wrote her approving letters and asked for her advice on New Age practices and beliefs. Many told her that she was writing about things they had believed for some time but had kept secret for fear of criticism.

MacLaine devoted much of *Out on a Limb* to her love affair with a married man, described in the book as a high-ranking English politician but later revealed to be a composite figure derived from two political leaders with whom she had affairs. The purpose of including this sordid tale comes to light later in the book when a channeler reveals to her that one of these men was married to her in a previous life in the lost city of Atlantis. Details of their relationship in this previous incarnation explain difficulties in their present relationship. MacLaine also believes that strong attraction to a person signifies a close relationship in a previous life.

The most interesting parts of the book describe her experiences with a person named David, later explained to be a composite figure representing four "spiritual people" who acted as her guides into the New Age. David invited her to meet him in a remote mountainous area of Peru, where, we are told, local people often see UFOs. He introduced her to meditation while bathing in a hot spring. After a few days of skeptical participation, MacLaine had an out-of-body experience while concentrating on the flame of a candle. She felt herself floating above the pool, attached to her physical body by a "thin, thin silver cord." In her own words:

I had read about the silver cord in metaphysical literature. It glistened in the air. It felt limitless in length . . . totally elastic, always attached to my body. My sight came from some kind of spiritual eye. It wasn't like seeing with real eyes. I soared higher and wondered how far the cord would stretch without snapping. The moment I thought about hesitation, my soaring stopped. I stopped my flight, consciously, in space. I didn't want to go any higher. As it was I could see the curvature of the Earth, and darkness on the other side of the globe. The space surrounding my spirit was soothing and gentle and pure.

New Age literature widely reports such out-of-body experiences. The need for a "silver cord" attaching body to spirit, however, is a matter of some disagreement. Another popular guru, Dick Sutphen, has derided the idea, saying one can go anywhere one wants in the spirit without such a cord and without the permission of spiritual entities—permission that others claim is necessary to avoid danger. MacLaine's out-of-body experience marks an important turning point. With such a personal and previously unthinkable experience, believing the other things she was being taught about the New Age perspective became much easier.

Out on a Limb was made into a film and shown as a television miniseries in early 1987 on the ABC network. Several episodes in this film were not in the book because, said MacLaine, readers were "not prepared then to believe." From a Christian perspective, the most shocking moment in the film is when David and Shirley stand on the beach near her Malibu home, stretch out their arms, and proclaim repeatedly with great confidence, "I am God." The series did not have high viewer ratings and received poor reviews; one reviewer called it "pervasive, paranormal poppycock." Nevertheless, New Age students place great significance on this television series. Some have even called it the single most important event in the growth of the New Age subculture.

Her next book, *Dancing in the Light*, remained on the *New York Times* best-seller list for thirty weeks and has sold over two million copies. One critic calls it "a droll mixture of egoism and altruism, intelligence and gullibility, curiosity and willful ignorance." This time the romantic interest focused on her affair with a Russian filmmaker called Vassily Okhlpol. "Vassy," as she calls him, also believes in reincarnation, but, because of his early Christian training, cannot give up his belief in evil and the existence of Satan. MacLaine, on the other hand, believes that there is no such thing as evil. What Christians call *evil*, she says, is only "energy flying backward." While *Out on a Limb* teaches that we are all co-creators with God, now she says that each individual person *is* God. Her spirit guides tell her that she and Vassy knew each other in past lives. They were good friends, she a man and he a woman.

In 1987, *It's All in the Playing* was released. Another best-seller, it has nevertheless been called her most boring autobiography, probably because it is essentially more of the same. The book ends with a vision she has of a large UFO and her assertion that she has now found the "Christ consciousness" in herself.

MacLaine continues to write books about New Age beliefs and practices, but now she has added yet another facet to her leadership in the movement. In 1987 she began to offer consciousness-raising seminars. Hotel ballrooms all over the country have been the "in" place to be seen with Shirley. A large proportion of those who come are wealthy, middle-aged women. Some people have reportedly spent most of a summer trailing her from one seminar to the next. These "Connecting with Higher Self" seminars are a $300 weekend course in which she teaches people that "to know the self is the only thing worth knowing." Only a change in our collective consciousness can save the earth from serious trouble. MacLaine says:

> All this is about the heart. . . . That's why I won't let people at my seminars take notes or tape record. They can get the stuff I'm telling them from any good metaphysical bookstore. This isn't new, but for me to have them access their hearts, so that they can go home and cook that breakfast from a brand-new perspective. . . . It was becoming clear to me that the bridge between the unseen and the seen was getting shorter and shorter

(and I) just wanted to explain that. . . . The crux of it all is that we're creating everything in our lives ourselves . . . the good and the bad.

In typical New Age style, MacLaine advises seminar participants that learning a great deal from books is not always helpful. "I became so educated in metaphysics that I actually became confused." MacLaine is not deterred by critics' suggestions that she is confused and understands little of what she has read. Better, she says, to concentrate on your own experience. Some people come away from such sessions claiming psychic healing, and MacLaine has been derided as a "New Age evangelist saving souls from the abyss."

In one summer tour, she took in an estimated almost four million dollars. Already wealthy, MacLaine has said she conducts these seminars in order to raise money for a spiritual center where people could come to study numerology, color therapy, channeling, reincarnation, and other New Age concepts in greater depth than weekend seminars allow. Lest one conclude this is all altruistic, however, she has also said, "I want to prove spirituality is profitable. . . . I've liked moderate success, but I've not wanted gigantic success. I'm changing now. I want gigantic success."

MacLaine was called a "popular guru for the eighties." *Time* magazine called her "the New Age's reigning whirling dervish," and journalist Russell Chandler in *Understanding the New Age* called her the "high priestess" of the New Age movement. She has succeeded enormously in New Age circles.

New Age Theology

Although much of what MacLaine professes as New Age learning resembles that of other New Age leaders, she leads the promotion of the New Age practice of channeling and the belief in absolute relativism.

Channeling

Rosemary Ellen Guiley in *Harper's Encyclopedia of Mystical and Paranormal Experience* defines channeling as "a form of mediumship in which information is communicated from a source perceived to be different from the conscious self. Sources are identified variously as nonphysical beings, angels, nature spirits, totem or guardian spirits, deities, demons, extraterrestrials, spirits of the dead, and the Higher Self. . . . As a New Age phenomenon, channeling has almost exclusively focused on the delivery of religious or spiritual information allegedly obtained from spiritual sources, such as highly evolved and nonphysical entities (who usually have exotic names), angels, Jesus, God, and the Virgin Mary."

Channeling now has many forms. The most popular in New Age practice is trance channeling, in which a person claims to be in a trance and unaware of the voice that is speaking through him or her. Others use methods such as automatic writing or a Ouija board. Many New Age beliefs have come through channelers—musical and artistic works are sold with the open assertion that they were channeled. Children in some classrooms are being taught to consult "spirit guides." Even Fritjof Capra, discussed in the next chapter, has said, "Sometimes while writing *The Tao of Physics*, I felt that it was being written through me, rather than by me. The subsequent events have confirmed these feelings."

Several channelers have maintained their popularity for years. Jane Roberts, who began her journey into the New Age experimenting with a Ouija board and soon was dispensing advice from Seth, was among the first. Kevin Ryerson benefited greatly from playing himself in the MacLaine television series and has introduced many to channeling since the late eighties. J. Z. Knight, also consulted by MacLaine, has been very popular, giving advice from Ramtha to many famous people in the entertainment industry.

MacLaine's book *Dancing in the Light* contains accounts of many sessions with channelers. In addition to the "entities" she contacts through Ryerson, she was also guided by Ramtha, channeled by Knight. Ramtha teaches there is no God separate from the universe, but only a supernatural force that holds everything together as part of the universe. Ramtha calls the Bible an "insidious book" because it has taught people to believe in hell and Satan. Knight's central teaching is that each person creates his or her own reality. If we can learn to love ourselves, we will have the power to be healthy and happy and to live forever.

One of the most unusual channelers is Helen Cohen Schucman, who in the late sixties, when she was a psychology professor at Columbia University and considered herself an atheist, heard a voice say, "This is a course in miracles. Please take notes." During a seven-year period, she recorded over one thousand pages of dictation, which have been published as *A Course in Miracles*, called a "self-study program for spiritual psychotherapy" and "a guide to the miraculous applications of love as a balm on every wound." According to Schucman, Jesus' apostles did not record his teachings correctly, so Jesus instructed her to act as his channel to the modern world. "The Course," as it is called, has become so popular that numerous study groups, including some in churches, meet all over the country. Many believe they are studying a form of Christianity. The teachings, far from Christian, include the belief that time, space, pain, death, illness, and sin are all illusions.

Probably the most popular and successful channeler in a business sense is Jach Pursel, who claims to channel an "entity" called Lazaris and has been consulted by many famous people, including Shirley MacLaine. Lazaris calls himself "content without form . . . a spark of consciousness that exists and is aware of its existence, that creates thought and creates reality." He says that 95 percent of the drugs doctors give are not proven to work and advocates self-healing by believing in oneself. Lazaris "eloquently holds forth on the use of color, auras, light, and sound as healing devices." He is described as "consistently funny, warm, and engaging . . . although half of what he says is nonsense." For example, he teaches that you can change a person's mood by shining a colored light on his or her picture—each color will evoke a particular mood. He "leads us into a Walt Disney World of innocence, free of misery and corruption" where "nature isn't cruel, hearts aren't broken, dreams don't die, and neither do we." Although there might be four hundred people at a Pursel weekend seminar, he takes a moment to speak to each one. "Instead of a Communion wafer, these devotees receive from Lazaris a crystal 'personally charged' just for them, nestled in a basket draped with blue velvet." In addition to his books, tapes, and seminars, Pursel earns huge sums from private telephone consultations.

What is really happening during a channeling session? Many immediately assume that all channelers are money-hungry frauds who make up these "channeled entities" and are good enough actors to convince gullible people. No doubt many frauds are among the channelers, but it seems doubtful that all are such.

One possibility is that some participants have psychological disorders. Most psychologists who have studied channeling consider it self-delusion. Studies have shown the spirits speaking through people tend to have characteristics similar to those people. The combination of a psychological problem and years of study of occult literature convinces some they are channeling nonphysical beings, when in fact they are only outwardly expressing some inner aberration. J. Z. Knight's messages, for example, reflect her experiences of abuse as a child.

Many New Age people themselves do not believe that channeling really involves contact with spiritual beings. Rather, they explain it as people gaining contact with their "higher self" or "oversoul" or "superconscious," which is not generally part of conscious thinking. New Agers' favorite psychiatrist, Carl Jung, suggested that another source of channeling might be the collective unconscious, what he hypothesized to be a common unconscious memory of the history of the human race. Others' more acceptable explanation is that even normal people can experience a form of self-hypnosis during which they believe they are channeling a spirit.

Some of those who have studied channeling, however, believe that although most of it can be explained as either fraud or a psychological problem, some cases cannot be easily dismissed. They argue that at least occasionally information is transmitted that the person speaking could not have known. A famous example is that of the English medium Eileen Garrett, who in 1930 reported technical and secret information—supposedly from airmen who had died in a dirigible crash. This case is presented in *The Airmen Who Would Not Die* by John G. Fuller, condensed in the June 1979 *Reader's Digest.*

An outsider would find it remarkable that people who reject the idea of a personal God or God-given laws for behavior eagerly accept direction from "nonphysical entities." Although they reject organized religion, they still feel a need for direction. As someone has said, "those who do not believe in God will believe anything."

Total Relativism

Relativism is common in modern societies where we deal daily with diverse beliefs and values. New Age thinking, however, has become totally relativistic. Chandler, with tongue in cheek, accurately calls it "absolute relativism." Generally relativism says that each society and subculture has the right to decide what is right and wrong for itself. New Agers have taken an additional giant step and assert that the individual person may decide this. Furthermore, New Agers declare that each person creates his or her own reality, deciding what is real for oneself—no reality exists beyond the individual. Anyone who names a universal truth is only trying to gain power over others. *Evil* is simply a word for a "lower form of consciousness." MacLaine says, "Until mankind realizes that there is, in truth, no God and there is, in truth, no evil, there will be no peace." Once such total relativism is absorbed, the focus of interest locks into the self. What else is left? So New Agers are forever finding themselves, getting in touch with themselves, seeking self-fulfillment and self-actualization. MacLaine says that "the most profound relationship we will ever have is the one with ourselves."

Even secular social scientists agreed long ago that extreme relativism makes no sense. If everyone really tried to live this way, society would cease to exist. Without a common reality, we would have no common ethics or morals. People like MacLaine cannot practice what they preach. People cannot possibly live together without common values and standards of conduct. MacLaine, like everyone else, constantly judges what is right and wrong in others' beliefs and behaviors. Her repeated attacks on Christianity make this obvious.

In *America: The Sorcerer's New Apprentice,* David Hunt and T. A. McMahon summarize Sir James Jeans's argument that three things we all experience do not fit with the idea that each person can create his or her own reality. The first is surprise. "Twenty million people are suddenly awakened from a sound sleep by an earthquake. The fact that so many people were surprised by this event, indeed awakened by the shaking and roaring of an earthquake that they certainly were not even dreaming of, is evidence enough that an objective reality imposed itself upon its victims." The second is the continuity of objective reality. "After a twenty-year absence you return to your high school for a reunion. The same rooms in which you once attended class are there, complete with desks, blackboards, and cracks in the ceiling—everything that you had never given a thought to during the twenty-year interval has remained in place without your mind supporting its existence." Finally he points to changes that occur without our knowledge. Returning for a high school reunion, you might find that "the old gymnasium has been torn down and a new and much larger one stands in its place. Change such as this . . . clearly has occurred without our minds creating it."

Although nobody else is of MacLaine's stature, many other celebrities discuss their experiences with reincarnation and other New Age themes on television talk shows. Apparently many in the public refuse to doubt "when the rich and famous say it's true." Reincarnation or channeling is a theme in some of the most popular releases, watched uncritically by many Christians in recent years: *Dead Again, Ghost, Defending Your Life,* and *The Butcher's Wife. Time* magazine says, "To some degree, the preoccupation with the afterlife reflects the obsession of Los Angeles, the crystal-and-channeling capital of the country, where people can mention their past lives with the same seriousness as getting the car engine tuned." A 1988 *Los Angeles Times* poll found that "Los Angeles women with household incomes above $40,000 are more likely to have been to a channeler than to a psychotherapist, psychiatrist, or counselor."

Los Angeles may have a high concentration of believers, but New Age has entered the mainstream of North American culture. A recent poll showed 14 percent of Americans believe in trance channeling. Stockbrokers and Wall Street raiders turn to channelers for advice. Today we can book a New Age vacation through a New Age travel agency or send our children to a New Age summer camp. The well-known Esalen Institute is only one of many holistic centers offering lectures, workshops, and retreats on New Age topics; courses by mail are available for everything from yoga to herbology. Magazine ads give phone numbers of psychics, astrologers, and numerologists. If not in the local New Age store, readily available by mail are New Age children's books, Ouija boards, do-it-yourself astrology software, and a host of products designed to enhance the psychic spirit, including incense, fetishes, and Zen shrines. Many commentators have pointed out the irony of a spiritual movement that has so quickly developed such highly materialistic dimensions.

Channeling and Relativism and the Christian

Someone passing out tracts at a New Age gathering asked a person if she was going to heaven. She replied that she did not understand the question, because it did not fit her concept of reality. She did not feel accountable to any higher power, but rather considered herself "a God of her own universe." MacLaine says, "I think each of us is the arbiter between ourselves and our own God. We make God in our own image." The blatantly anti-Christian nature of this thinking becomes painfully evident in *Dancing in the Light*, where MacLaine says that she is "part of the God source" and therefore can say of herself, "I AM that I AM." Thus she takes to herself the name God gives himself in the Old Testament. Although the monism of Eastern religion shares the belief that God is everywhere and thus in everyone, it would reject this idea of making God in one's own image. In Eastern religion the individual person is really nothing but illusion—hardly the center of one's own universe.

Channelers' central message is that of monism and the inherent goodness and power of the self. There is no sin, no need for forgiveness, no need for a Savior. Whatever a person's problem, it results from lack of understanding of self or alienation from self. The solution is to work on the problem by finding what is best for the individual.

If—and skepticism seems in order here—some cases of channeling cannot be dismissed as fake or psychological problems, how are we to explain this practice? Some Christian students of channeling believe that meditation can open a person up to demonic influence. Says one, "Of the channelers and psychics I have studied, nearly every one first came in contact with his or her spirit guide while practicing some form of Eastern meditation." Some have reported "bad trips" involving meetings with what can be described as demonic forces. Channeling is not, as New Agers claim, the same as inspired prophecy in the Bible. Quite the opposite. Although some profess to channel Jesus, their teachings oppose the teachings of Scripture and must be rejected (1 John 2:18-29; 4:1-3). In fact, Scripture warns us repeatedly against consulting spirits. If any actual spirits are channeled, they can be only satanic in origin (Deut. 18:9-22; Isa. 8:16-20; Acts 16:16-18).

The self-centeredness of New Age thinking involves what has often been called the most deadly of sins: the sin of pride. New Age relativism has been likened to the serpent's claim in Genesis 3:5 that people "knowing good and evil" could decide for themselves what is right and wrong. The atheist says Christianity is untrue; the New Age's relativism claims that it may be part of the Christian reality, but it is not part of New Age reality. Life teaches us that we cannot control reality, much less create our own reality. We must bend to reality, not the reverse. C. S. Lewis says that "all reality is iconoclastic"—evidence that you and I are not God.

The Bible teaches that God commands us to love him and to love our neighbor. We find our self-worth in knowing he created us in his image and loves us. Nowhere are we told that the central focus of our lives should be self-love and self-development. In fact, we are directly warned against trusting our inner self (Jer. 17:5-9; Mark 7:14-23). Paul says we should be self-effacing and think of others before ourselves. If Christ humbled himself "to assume the condition of a slave" (Phil. 2:1-11), who are we to assert our self-interest? James tells us to live by "the wisdom that comes down from above," not by looking within ourselves for wisdom (James 3:15-17).

Suggestions for Group Session

Getting Started

Christians could easily dismiss MacLaine as eccentric, even insane as her critics often describe her. But somehow we have to reconcile her "blatantly anti-Christian" stance with her tremendous influence on the Hollywood film industry, in the lives of affluent Americans (especially women), and on the mainstream of North American culture. One more MacLaine joke will not refute the success of her New Age religion.

MacLaine's account of her search for self is as old as the story of Adam and Eve, who "early in human history . . . listened to the intruder's voice. Rather than living by the Creator's word of life, they fell for Satan's lie and sinned. They forgot their place; they tried to be like God." When "looking for life without God, we find only death; grasping for freedom outside his law, we trap ourselves in Satan's snares;

pursuing pleasure, we lose the gift of joy" (*Our World Belongs to God,* 14, 15).

Begin this session with a prayer of thanksgiving to God for his work of grace in our lives, and thanking him that he kept his promise to Adam and Eve to send a Savior. Praise him for his gift of love and joy.

Group Discussion and Activity

1. Read 1 John 2:18-23. John is warning us about the antichrists. "John assumed his readers knew that a great enemy of God and his people will arise before Christ's return. That person is called 'antichrist.' . . . But prior to him, there will be many antichrists . . . [who will] deny the incarnation and that Jesus is the divine Christ . . . deny the Father . . . do not have the Father . . . are liars and deceivers . . . are many . . . left the church because they had nothing in common with believers" (The *NIV Study Bible* notes for 1 John 2:18). Do any of these descriptions of the antichrists portray the New Age leaders we have been discussing? How timely is this warning today?

2. 2 Thessalonians 2:4 warns about "the man of lawlessness." "He will oppose and will exalt himself over everything that is called God or is worshipped, so that he sets himself up in God's temple, proclaiming himself to be God." Can this warning assess the thinking of Shirley MacLaine and other New Age leaders?

3. Deuteronomy 18:9-22 and Isaiah 8:19-22 warn about consulting spirits. What do these passages say to the Christian about channeling?

4. Read 2 Thessalonians 2:9-12. The *NIV Matthew Henry Commentary* explains verse 11 and 12 in these words:

   An erroneous mind and vicious life often go together and help forward one another. [God] will punish men for their unbelief, and for their dislike of the truth and love for sin and wickedness. He sometimes withdraws his grace from such sinners . . . he gives them up to their own hearts' lusts, and leaves them to themselves, and then sin will follow naturally.

   How does this explanation contrast with MacLaine's declaration, "Until mankind realizes that there is, in truth, no God and there is, in truth, no evil, there will be no peace"?

5. New Age relativism seems to contradict itself. Following are some questions you might ask a New Ager. (You might wish to break in-

to smaller groups to sort through the logic of the New Age thinking. Imagine that you are actually asking one of the questions and expecting an answer. How would a New Ager respond? How would you refute their reasoning? Share your conclusions with the entire group.)

- If total relativism is correct, how can Christianity be wrong or in any way inferior to New Age teachings?
- If total relativism is correct, how can racism, sexism, environmental exploitation (or anything else) be wrong?
- If a person is God, why is it necessary to improve oneself? Does God need improving?
- If a person suddenly becomes aware that he or she is God, does God grow in knowledge? How can God be unaware of his own existence?
- How does the idea that there is no distinction between good and bad fit with the New Age idea that humanity is evolving toward a higher (better) form?

6. In what sense is the Christian's self-love and self-esteem different from MacLaine's "profound relationship" with self? How can we be sure we are modeling and our children are learning a biblical self-concept in a society so centered on self?

7. Do you agree that "it is simply impossible for people to live together without some commonly held values and standards of conduct, some feeling that certain things are wrong no matter who does them"? Imagine what would happen without stop signs, work schedules, product standards, graduation requirements, church membership criteria, and so on.

Closing

Close this session by reading together these words from 1 John 2:24-29:

> *Stay with what you heard from the beginning, the original message. Let it sink into your life. If what you heard from the beginning lives deeply in you, you will live deeply in both Son and Father. This is exactly what Christ promised: eternal life, real life!*

> *I've written to warn you about those who are trying to deceive you. But they're no match for what is embedded deeply within you—Christ's anointing, no less! You don't need any of their so-called teaching. Christ's anointing teaches you the truth on*

everything you need to know about yourself and him, uncontaminated by a single lie. Live deeply in what you were taught.

—THE MESSAGE

Pray together for the Spirit's help to live deeply.

SIX

THE NEW SCIENCE EXPERIENCED BY FRITJOF CAPRA

Fritjof Capra, a sixties hippie and now noted author and physicist, is credited by critics with the "shotgun wedding" of physics and mysticism—the new science with monism at the heart. As we've analyzed the beliefs and practices of New Age leaders, we must conclude that nothing else taught by the New Age movement is more central, basic, and seductive than monism. Fritjof Capra is a captive leader.

Capra's Journey to New Age

Early Influences

Little in Fritjof Capra's childhood years in Austria would suggest that he would one day become a New Age guru. He has said that he came from a spiritual family and from childhood was always a very "spiritual person." Rejecting his parents' Catholicism, he looked elsewhere for meaning in his life.

In 1958, as a nineteen-year-old university student, Capra read *Physics and Philosophy* by Werner Heisenberg, one of the major theorists of modern physics. This book, he said, greatly influenced him. He gained intense interest in the complex questions and paradoxes introduced by atomic physics in the early part of the twentieth century. For years he dedicated himself to the study of physics, first classical physics and later quantum mechanics and relativity theory.

Following his postdoctoral research in theoretical physics at the University of Vienna, he was appointed to the University of California at Santa Cruz as a physics instructor. He arrived in California in 1968, a year one commentator recently marked as the beginning of the "culture wars." This also became an important turning point in Fritjof Capra's life. He himself later stated that during this time he "experienced the most profound and most radical personal transformation"—a period of "transpersonal expansion, the questioning of authority, a sense of empowerment, and the experience of sensuous beauty and community."

Capra was strongly attracted to the sixties counterculture and began to live a "schizophrenic life . . . part-time postdoctoral research fellow and part-time hippie." He became involved in "rock festivals, the psychedelics, the new sexual freedom, the communal living, the many days on the road." He reports, "I spent many nights in my sleeping bag on secluded beaches, solitary days in meditation high up in the hills."

Late in 1968, Capra attended a series of lectures by J. Krishnamurti, a popular Indian teacher who had strongly influenced the thinking of David Bohm, a better-known physicist. Krishnamurti presented a largely Buddhist view of reality, encouraging his listeners to solve their problems by "going beyond thought, beyond language, beyond time . . . to achieve freedom from the known." Capra was so impressed that he seriously considered giving up physics to "leave reasoning behind." He arranged an introduction to Krishnamurti, who told him, "First you are a human being, then you are a scientist. First you have to become free, and this freedom cannot be achieved through thought. It is achieved through meditation—understanding the totality of life in which every form of fragmentation has ceased." Capra was convinced he could become a better scientist if he learned to be free, but Krishnamurti didn't explain how to do that.

On the beach at Santa Cruz during the summer of 1969, Capra experienced something to which he often referred. The opening passage of his first book, *The Tao of Physics*, describes this experience.

> *I was sitting by the ocean . . . watching the waves rolling in and feeling the rhythm of my breathing, when I suddenly became aware of my whole environment as being engaged in a gigantic cosmic dance. Being a physicist, I knew that the sand, rocks, water and air around me were made of vibrating molecules and atoms, and that these consisted of particles which interacted with one another by creating and destroying other particles. . . . But until that moment I had only experienced it through graphs, diagrams and mathematical theories. As I sat on that beach my*

> *former experiences came to life; I "saw" cascades of energy coming down from outer space . . .; I "saw" the atoms of the elements and those of my body participating in this cosmic dance of energy; I felt its rhythm and I heard its sound, and at that moment I knew that this was the Dance of Shiva, the Lord of Dancers worshipped by the Hindus.*

Thus Capra's study of Eastern mysticism and his practice of meditation led to a life-changing event, which convinced him of the truth of the monistic perspective of Eastern religion.

Career Paths

In 1970, Capra's visa expired and he returned to Europe in search of a research fellowship at a major university. He settled in London for the next four years, a period he has called a "difficult transition." The difficulty included a series of separations from his wife; they eventually divorced. Also because his interest in developing a science with a social conscience through the relationship of Eastern religion and physics dominated his life, he was unwilling to take on a full-time position in teaching or research.

Working at various part-time research jobs in research and teaching to make enough money to sustain himself, he spent as much time as possible on what he called his "vision." Of the various Eastern traditions, he found himself most interested in Taoism because it "offers the most profound and most beautiful expressions of ecological wisdom, emphasizing both the fundamental oneness of all phenomena and embeddedness of individuals and societies in the cyclical processes of nature." In the spring of 1971, his first article, "The Dance of Shiva: the Hindu View of Matter in the Light of Modern Physics," was published in the journal *Main Currents in Modern Thought*. He gave papers on this topic to gatherings of physicists in Austria and Geneva, but he found them "hardly more than polite, slightly amused." He was strongly encouraged, however, by a visit in Munich with his hero, Heisenberg, who agreed with him completely.

Deciding to take the plunge and commit himself fully to his vision, Capra wrote the first three chapters of his book, *The Tao of Physics*. In order to understand the mystical view of Eastern religion, he began to practice meditation regularly. He wanted to understand what he was investigating "not only intellectually but also at a deeper level through intuitive insight."

At the end of 1974, the book was finished and Capra returned to California to await its publication and further develop his ideas. Probably because of his unorthodox view, he never gained a research or teaching position at any major university. He spent most of his time on broader research that "transcends the narrow confines of current academic disciplines... trying to push (the limits of science) outward into new areas... too novel and controversial to be supported by any academic institution." Looking back on his work some years later, he recognized a consistent theme: "the fundamental change of world view that is occurring in science and in society, the unfolding of a new vision of reality, and the social implications of this cultural transformation."

In April of 1975, Capra was invited to work as an unpaid member of a physics research team headed by an outstanding physicist, Geoffrey Chew. He had been involved in this research group on and off for many years. According to Capra, he had developed a close relationship with Chew, and Capra clearly admired Chew, calling him a "truly original thinker." At one point, he remarked that "although he [Chew] considers himself a Christian and is close to the Catholic tradition, I cannot help feeling that his approach to life shows, basically, a Buddhist attitude." Apparently Capra found it difficult to reconcile his admiration for Chew with Chew's Christianity.

A New Age Leader

The Tao of Physics: An Exploration of the Parallels Between Modern Physics and Eastern Mysticism was released in 1975. The established scientific community paid little attention, but it created an immediate sensation among the thousands in the growing New Age community. Since first publication, it has gone through two more editions, been translated into over a dozen languages, and sold over a million copies worldwide. Its growing popularity brought some critical reviews, most calling it interesting but largely unconvincing. Nevertheless, the book is now considered a "New Age classic." Capra has been invited to lecture about his ideas to many audiences in North America, Europe, and Asia. Earnings from the book and lectures freed Capra to continue his exploration.

In brief summary, Capra argues in *The Tao of Physics* that ancient mystics (both East and West, but most clearly in the East) understood the nature of reality that twentieth century physics is in the process of verifying scientifically. At the heart of this teaching lies monism, the belief that all is one; that no distinction exists between Creator and creation, between spirit and matter; that all matter is alive; and the cosmos is one living being.

With the popular acceptance of *The Tao of Physics,* Capra began to travel widely, lecturing and participating in conferences on "new thinking." He became convinced that what he had described in his book was part of a larger social change. He believed that a "profound cultural transformation," a "change of consciousness," is in process in Europe and North America. People fear that human survival is being threatened, and this calls for "new-paradigm thinking," a holistic and ecological worldview that recognizes the fundamental oneness of everything.

Capra was right about one thing. Many people saw things as he did. A loose network of people and organizations formed to promote this new paradigm, outlined in a 1980 book by Marilyn Ferguson, *The Aquarian Conspiracy*. In this popular work, sometimes called "the New Age bible," Ferguson refers to and draws some of her ideas from Capra to support her contention that the "new science" is "confirming paradoxes and intuitions humankind has come across many times but stubbornly disregarded. It is telling us that our social institutions and our very ways of existence violate nature." The demand for "personal and social transformation" was growing. Capra was in the forefront, a leader in what Ferguson in 1976 called "the movement that has no name," but what was soon called the "aquarian conspiracy," and most commonly now the "New Age Movement."

To develop his idea that the new physics was but part of a more general ongoing culture change, Capra threw himself into an intensive study of how the new thinking was influencing biology and medicine, psychology, and economics. Capra realized his error in arguing that physics should be the model for change in other disciplines. Instead, he concluded that physics was but one special and important example of a more general shift in thinking to what is called the systems approach. The systems view concentrates on interrelations and interdependence. Capra believes that anything we study is "merely one aspect of a whole ecological and social fabric; a living system composed of human beings in continual interaction with one another and with their natural resources, most of which are, in turn, living organisms."

In 1977 Capra came upon what he thought was a "profound connection between ecology and spirituality." He considered that an ecological approach might "become our Western equivalent of the Eastern mystical traditions." While many discussed the need to be holistic, Capra thought that an ecological approach was even broader and more inclusive.

The next year he joined the ecological movement with radical feminism and enthusiastically supported eco-feminism, the movement that integrates ecology and feminism. To him, feminist thinking was more in keeping with a holistic and ecological view; the "radical feminist critique [had] a strong intellectual fascination" for him. Western culture had become too patriarchal, and he believed this was at least partly the consequence of the dominance of Christianity in Western society. Christianity teaches a "male god" while other traditions include various goddess figures to allow for the expression of the female side in religion. He approved of the return of the goddess image and predicted that the women's movement would play an important role in the emergence of the new culture.

Capra worked hard on his new ideas, traveling extensively to consult with various people, experimenting with meditation techniques, and fasting for several days at a time. He "began to see the body as a whole, as a reflection or manifestation of the psyche." Thus he came to the common New Age view that, although all is one, somehow the spiritual is more basic than the material. He began to try out the behavioral implications of what he was working on at a theoretical level. "I adopted a regular discipline of relaxation and physical exercise, changed my diet and cleansed my body twice a year with fruit-juice fasts, practiced preventive heath care through chiropractic and other bodywork techniques, worked with my dreams, and experienced the broad range of therapeutic techniques I was investigating." All this convinced him that "the process of getting sick and of healing are essentially mental processes." He also became convinced that meditation was a great aid to working efficiently.

In February of 1979, some of those whom Capra considered his most valuable advisors were invited to a three-day discussion at an estate in the Big Sur area of California. None of them had ever met before, yet, according to Capra, they were all "fascinated again and again to discover how our ideas interconnected." They agreed that despite their many differences, all were part of a minority culture rising to challenge the declining majority culture. Manifestations of this new culture included the popularity of jogging, health-food stores, new schools of thought in psychology, and the feminist and ecology movements.

Capra's second book, *The Turning Point*, was published in 1982. It begins with a quotation from an ancient Chinese work, the *I Ching:* "After a time of decay comes the turning point. . . . The old is discarded and the new is introduced." The thesis of the book, Capra says, is that we live in a time of "crisis of perception." Disintegrating western culture desperately needs a new vision, a new paradigm. The old view, called the *Cartesian-Newtonian* view, offers us nature as an object to exploit. It has caused many of the "diseases of civilization," such as heart disease, cancer, strokes, depression, schizophrenia, inflation, unemployment, and poverty. It lies at the root of the current dangers to the ecosystem, such as air and water pollution. Once people recognize they share this new paradigm, they will unite into a powerful holistic, ecological movement. This movement will bring individual healing, solve social problems, and improve the natural environment.

The call for active involvement in social change, so strong a theme in *The Turning Point*, becomes even stronger in Capra's next book, *Green Politics*, co-authored by Sharlene Spretnak. This book about the worldwide green movement received almost no reviews and rapidly sank into obscurity. Capra had been hoping for this moment, which he called a "coalescence of ecology, peace, and feminist movements." Apparently, though, most of the people who were intrigued by Capra's earlier ideas had little or no interest in the green ideas.

Capra's next book was a reflective work called *Uncommon Wisdom*. In this book he tells the "personal story behind the evolution of my ideas" and the "encounters with many remarkable men and women who inspired me, helped me, and supported my search." This book also sparked little public interest.

In 1991 Capra published *Belonging to the Universe* with David Steindel-Rast and Thomas Matus, Catholic priests. This book simply records conversations of Capra, Steindel-Rast, and Mast at a conference at the Esalen Institute in California, a mecca for New Age intellectuals and one of Capra's favorite places. This book exemplifies how New Age people attempt to incorporate Christianity into their scheme of things. In much of this book, the two priests try to convince Capra that Christianity and Buddhism are "perfectly compatible when rightly understood." They do this by altering Christianity into something that will better fit Oriental mysticism. Capra repeatedly points to Christian doctrines that are inconsistent with mystical monism, and the priests repeatedly claim that "new-paradigm theology" has changed all that into something compatible. They make statements such as these:

- "Salvation really means realizing your connection to the whole of the universe, your experience of being at home, feeling secure, truly belonging in some ultimate sense."
- "Jesus himself was a mystic."
- "The Kingdom of God is our belonging to this great cosmic reality."
- "God became human in order that every human being may become God."

This illustrates the New Age opinion that all religions are valuable and ultimately compatible. Capra, to his credit, seems reluctant to participate in this revisionist theology and is much more skeptical than most of his friends that Christianity can fit his Eastern mysticism. Yet, he apparently backed off somewhat from his total rejection of Christianity.

The last report we have of Capra was in 1992 upon the release of a film called *Mindwalk*, for which he co-wrote the screenplay. This film has been compared to another, *My Dinner with Andre*, because both discuss New Age ideas. In this case, the discussion involves three characters. One, a physicist played by Liv Ullmann, represents Capra and expounds his ideas. There appears to be a deliberate avoidance of discussion of Eastern religion, with only one passing reference to the god Shiva. The emphasis is on systems theory and the need for ecological awareness and changes in policy. One reviewer commented, "I like the total philosophy of Capra, and I think it would do everyone a lot of good to be introduced to it." One can only wonder if the average viewer, or even the average reviewer, understands the monistic, anti-Christian message Capra projects. Like other New Age material, it leads us to think we are being exposed to an innocuous, probably secular, but possibly Christian worldview.

The New Age New Science

New Science centers on monism. Other characteristics of the New Science movement common throughout the entire New Age movement include the great respect for Eastern religions, the mystical approach to science, and the emphasis on ecological environmentalism.

Monism at the Heart

The New Age movement is not simply a few foreign practices such as channeling, crystal healing, or meditation. Most New Age people are engaged in at least one or more such practices, arguing that the only way to understand reality is through *experiencing* a "higher state" of being—but what gives such practices meaning? Although New Age people are diverse and claim open minds, they unite in their monistic view of the world.

Monism says God is not a personal being, but rather a sort of impersonal force that holds the universe together. God is in everything, and everything is God. Each person is God and can create one's own reality. The biblical idea of sin is rejected in favor of a private morality—the problem with the world is not sin, but ignorance. Curing the ills of the world requires teaching new ways of thinking.

To Capra, God is not a separate, personal being, but rather "the self-organizing dynamics of the entire cosmos." Self-organization, also called the *cosmic dance*, is Capra's way of explaining the order he sees about him. The universe began in the chaos of the big bang but is gradually evolving toward greater order and greater complexity. Although he believes this can be explained and defended on a logical basis, he also believes that the best way to understand the nature of the universe is to use the approach of many ancient mystics, that is, some form of meditation in which "all the boundaries and dualism have been transcended, and all individuality dissolves into universal, undifferentiated oneness."

The last days of the twentieth century present a conflict between three basic views of the world. Christians are familiar with two of these: the Christian view of a world created and sustained by a personal God, and the secular view that the universe is strictly material and nonspiritual. But changes in popular culture show that New Age spiritual monism is now rapidly gaining popularity. Books, music, films, and television are increasingly enamored of this new teaching. While Christians fight secularism, a new paganism invades our society. As Chad Walsh once said, "The Bible devotes remarkably little time to the menace of atheism. The biblical viewpoint seems to be that atheism is a rare and puny adversary compared to idolatry." Certainly this is what we find in the New Age movement—a resurgence of an old idolatry.

Sociologist Robert Bellah claims that many people in North American society now have a "vague spiritual orientation"—they have grown dissatisfied with secularism. While this situation can be an opportunity for Christianity to bring in new converts, it is also an opportunity for New Age thinking to expand. Some now argue that the New Age is even "creeping into Christian thought and more than a few churches." Thus, the near future of western society seems to hold a growing confrontation between Christian theism and New Age monism.

Idealized Oriental Spirituality

Capra has been accused of misinterpreting Asian religions and cultures "on almost every page" of *The Tao of Physics*. He seems to have created "an idealized Oriental spirituality—an idealized image against which to critique the perceived deficiencies of the West." One expert on the Orient calls the East "a convenient screen on which the West projects reverse images of its own deficiencies." This romanticizing of the East was common long before the sixties counterculture movement. The nineteenth century transcendentalist movement led by such luminaries as Emerson and Thoreau was particularly instrumental in influencing Westerners to think in terms of a materialistic West contrasted with a spiritual East. The New Age movement, with Capra in the lead, has picked up this theme and developed it as never before.

Although Capra admires many aspects of Eastern religions, the most significant to him is monism, the belief that the distinctions we make among God, ourselves, and nature are illusionary abstractions and that we can overcome this basic misunderstanding of the universe by "centering" the mind through meditation. In meditation, he believes, the basic oneness of everything is revealed experientially. Through meditation one can "transcend this realm of intellectual concepts" and realize that "good and bad are merely two sides of the same reality; extreme parts of a single whole."

Among the Eastern religions that teach monism, Capra especially admires Taoism because a "mistrust of conventional knowledge and reasoning is stronger in Taoism than in any other school of Eastern philosophy." This characteristic would appeal to counterculture people who certainly mistrusted convention. Taoism also emphasizes the integration of opposites into one whole, including the ideas of good and bad. Today, the Taoist symbol for the balance between yin (female) and yang (male) is common among the many T-shirt profundities found on the average American street, and popular films such as *The Dark Crystal* introduce our children at an early age to this "balance" of good and evil.

Capra supports such a view with modern physics' conception of the universe as a dynamic process that can, paradoxically, manifest itself as either energy or matter. Physics now shows us a reality that language cannot express, a reality that combines apparent opposites. Like Taoism, it unifies what seems incompatible into one on a "non-ordinary level of reality" where time and space become one dimension, and energy and matter become different ways to look at the same thing.

Capra admits that the relationship between ancient Eastern religion and modern physics, which he has argued so persuasively, "cannot be demonstrated conclusively but has to be experienced in a direct intuitive way." Sometime after *The Tao of Physics* was published, he said in an interview:

> *I can assert very sincerely that I have experienced all the similarities between physics and mysticism that I talk about in the book, at a level that is much deeper than an intellectual level. . . . This may sound like an unusual argument coming from a scientist, but it is not. You see in our culture these intuitive aspects of scientific discovery or any other kind of discovery are just not emphasized. But physicists know them very well.*

Here Capra hits on an idea of a variety of techniques of "enlightenment," an idea often heard from New Age proponents. Zen meditation, biofeedback, channeling, crystals, out-of-body experiences, and firewalking all claim that experience is the ultimate proof. This argument is difficult to answer. In fact, Christians also may say, "I cannot prove the existence of God abstractly, but I know from experience that he is real and that he loves me." Most of us will never understand particle physics well enough to decide experientially whether it closely relates to Eastern religious philosophies. Certainly many physicists have disagreed with Capra on this point.

Although Capra and other New Age thinkers greatly respect Eastern mysticism, they do not embrace it entirely. Its foreignness does not fit well in North American culture, so New Agers tend to borrow selectively from Eastern ideas and revise them to fit their own Western thinking. The New Age movement has many roots, but the entire movement is an adaptation of Eastern ideas to Western culture. For example, the Eastern view of history as cyclical is largely discarded for an evolutionary perspective. The Western importance of the individual wins out over the Eastern emphasis on the group. The claim that nothing is new in the New Age is not entirely true. Any particular belief or practice may well be traceable to a previous source, but the combination does indeed form something new. So in the New Age we see a new eclectic vision that has borrowed from many sources, Eastern mysticism being the most prominent.

Scientific Mysticism

Much has been made of the New Age dislike for science and technology. Many New Age people contend that in their "altered states of consciousness" they have found a better way to knowledge and understanding. But an increasingly popular view of a new science, in which Capra is clearly a leader, fits well with mysticism. Many in the New Age movement claim that what they learn through their meditation and other New Age practices is just as scientific as anything in the traditional laboratory. Much of this "new science," however, does not meet the traditional requirements of science. According to critics, the new science . . .

- is not skeptical.
- is not testable.
- is often incompatible with existing knowledge.
- ignores data that does not agree with it.
- is based almost entirely on personal experience.

Christian theism provided the environment in which science developed and thrived. Many scientists have rejected that Christian background for a purely secular view. But what does the future hold if the "new science" continues to gain ground?

Ecological Environmentalism

Capra argues strongly that we must reject the Cartesian view of nature as a structure of separate things that we can exploit; we must accept the older view of the earth as "a kind of nurturing mother, wild and uncontrollable." He blames the Christian tradition for our current problems. In the Christian view, he says, nature is governed by laws established by God. "The physical phenomena themselves were not thought to be divine in any sense, and when science made it more and more difficult to believe in such a god, the divine disappeared completely from the scientific world view, leaving behind the spiritual vacuum that has become characteristic of the mainstream of our culture."

In Capra's own monistic opinion, nature and god are made of one cloth, unaffected by outside laws. The ecological system must be understood spiritually. He finds this view more common in Eastern religion than in Christianity; he praises American Indian religion for its "intuitive wisdom" about nature. To Capra, the universe "can be understood only as patterns of cosmic process" as described in Taoism. Nothing about any person or any part of nature is independent of its environment.

Capra concluded that "the environment is not only alive but also mindful, like ourselves." "Individual human minds are embedded in the larger minds of social and ecological systems, and these are integrated into the planetary mental system . . . which in turn must participate in some kind of universal or cosmic mind." He distinguishes between "shallow environmentalism" and "the deep ecology movement" and rejects any environmentalism that does not involve a basic change in religion, a change to a monistic view of the oneness of nature.

The New Science and the Christian

With its underlying foundations in monism, the New Science movement leaves little doubt as to its anti-Christian teaching. New Age monists believe that they are taking part in an evolutionary development that will change the world for the better. From a Christian perspective, the wholeness the New Ager is seeking does not and cannot exist anywhere, since, because of sin, the world is broken. Such wholeness is yet to be established in the coming kingdom of God.

A monistic view of God as a life force excludes the possibility of worship. How can one thank a basic force? How can one love a force? How can it love us? New Agers emphasize love, but this love tends to focus on self, since no personal God is out there to love. Perhaps the most common theme in New Age literature is that we must learn to love ourselves. Loving others is at best a secondary theme. No mention is made of loving God. The grace of God does not fit either, since grace implies a personal relationship with God that is absent in New Age thinking.

Non-Christian scientists often profess that they must be dealing with something beyond or behind the surface reality. They may even refer to God, as Einstein did when he said that God does not play dice with the universe. But they are not expressing belief in a creator God. Often they are referring to something much closer to the New Age idea of an impersonal vital force.

Those who believe in a Creator God will interpret the findings of modern physics differently than Capra. The mystery and the complexity of nature support Christians' belief in a Creator. Romans 1:20 says, "For since the creation of the world God's invisible qualities—his eternal power and divine nature—have been clearly seen, being understood from what has been made, so that men are without excuse." Psalm 19:1 says, "The heavens declare the glory of God; the skies proclaim the work of his hands."

Yet Capra and many others argue that Christianity is anti-environmental. Their argument seems often to be built more on the poor environmental record of Christian societies than on any explicit Christian teachings. Some argue, however, that the Genesis command to "subdue the earth" is anti-environmental because it suggests the earth is something to be exploited rather than revered as a living being. Also, the Christian emphasis on the salvation of the individual person leads people to pay little attention to the natural world, while Eastern religion sees everything as interconnected and all nature as full of sacred, spiritual beings.

Environmental concerns and respect for nature are commendable, but New Age people have gone too far. Capra and other New Age teachers tell us that nature can do no wrong. Everything would be in perfect balance without the disruption of people. This reverence for nature is misplaced; Scripture teaches that sin has invaded not only the human heart but all of nature. Nature is full of pain, disease, and death. "Right thinking" is not going to change that.

Tony Campolo, in his recent book *How to Rescue the Earth Without Worshipping Nature*, suggests how Christians can be environmentally responsible without being drawn into New Age thinking. That seems once more to be the issue for the Christian, not only in regard to environmentalism but in response to the entire New Age movement. Where do we draw the line?

Suggestions for Group Session

Getting Started

As we conclude this series of discussions on New Age leaders, we can identify a variety of practices that seem to characterize most New Agers. Mysticism, alien visits, auditing, reincarnation, holistic health, evolution of humanity, channeling, meditation, a cosmic environmentalism—these underlying beliefs and practices are common threads woven in varying combinations throughout the lives of the six leaders we've studied. All New Agers are guided by their belief in monism.

Douglas Groothiuis in *Unmasking the New Age* defines monism as "the belief that all that is, is one. All is interrelated, interdependent and inter-penetrating. Ultimately there is no difference between God, a person, a carrot or a rock. They are all part of one continuous reality that has no boundaries, no ultimate divisions." This New Age monistic view conflicts with the Biblical teachings about . . .

- Jesus as the Son of God,
- Christ's resurrection and second coming,
- the distinction between good and evil,
- the believer's resurrection and eternal life,
- the need for a personal relationship with Jesus Christ,
- the commands to love God and our neighbor,
- the grace of God,
- the Creator God.

Knowing that this monistic view permeates New Age thinking, where do we draw the line? Can any part of Capra's thinking—and that of the other New Age gurus—withstand the scrutiny of the word of God? Or is New Age thinking seducing us?

The following discussion questions and activities are designed to help your group sort through Capra's New Science beliefs and summarize the influence of the larger New Age movement on our culture. This study was meant to increase our awareness of the seductive nature of the movement and equip us to respond with a biblical, Reformed perspective—less out of fear, more out of faith.

Begin this session with a prayer to thank God for the revelation of God the Father, Son, and Holy Spirit found in the Bible. Ask for an increased measure of faith to believe and stand firm in what we have been taught.

Group Discussion and Activity

1. As you've studied the lives of each of these six New Age leaders, were you struck by the fact that each was searching for meaning in life? Have you experienced this searching? What drew you to the God of the Bible? (You may wish to discuss these questions with a partner rather than with the entire group.)

2. Most of these New Age leaders, including Capra, rejected the beliefs of their parents. What challenges does this present to Christian parents today? How can the larger Christian community support parents in their responsibility to ground covenant children in the faith?

3. Read Psalm 19. How does the psalmist's relationship with God differ from the New Ager's idea of an impersonal vital force?

4. *Our World Belongs to God*, 4, says:

   Our world has fallen into sin;
   but rebellion and sin can never dethrone God.
   He does not abandon the work of his hand;
   the heavens still *declare his glory.*

   When have you been especially aware of the effects of sin on the world (the environment) God created? Are New Agers right to blame Christians for exploiting the earth in response to the command to "subdue the earth"? When have you recently praised God for the heaven's declaration and shown this praise in your response to reclaim God's creation? (For further study of this issue, your group may wish to use Calvin DeWitt's *Earth-Wise*, another book in the Issues in Christian Living series. This book, available from CRC Publications, gives a biblical response to environmental issues.)

5. Popular writer Virginia Ramey Mollenkott, who considers herself an evangelical Christian, says in a May, 1993, letter to *Christianity Today* that she learned monism from the Bible. "How else," she asks, "do you explain such passages as Ephesians 4:6, which tells of 'one God and Father of all, who is above all, and through all, and in you all'?" Read Ephesians 4:1-6 and compare Paul's description of unity in the body of Christ with Groothuis's definition of monism. What would you say to Mollenkott?

6. If indeed Christianity (along with the New Age movement) has an opportunity to reach the "many people in North American society [who] now have a 'vague spiritual orientation,'" what role can our churches play to reach these people? How can your congregation

identify them in your local community? How can we reach them with the gospel when New Age seems to have invaded every aspect of our culture?

7. Apparently Capra "began to back off from his total rejection of Christianity." Is it possible to be neutral toward Christ? Toward New Age? Weigh your response with the words of Luke 12:23.

8. Where do you personally draw the line on New Age thinking? (Break into small groups of two or three to discuss this final question. Be open to each other's struggles. Share your conclusions with the larger group.)

Closing

In 2 Thessalonians 2:6-8, Paul reminds us that "the time will come when the Antichrist will no longer be held back, but will be let loose. But don't worry. The Master Jesus will be right on his heels and blow him away" (*THE MESSAGE*). Paul adds these words of assurance in verses 13-14:

Meanwhile, we've got our hands full continually thanking God for you, our good friends—so loved by God! God picked you out as his from the very start. Think of it: included in God's original plan of salvation by the bond of faith in the living truth. This is the life of the Spirit he invited you to through the Message we delivered, in which you get in on the glory of our Master, Jesus Christ.

—THE MESSAGE

Conclude this session with a circle prayer time to reflect the final words in this passage (2 Thess. 2:15-16):

So, friends, take a firm stand, feet on the ground and head high. Keep a tight grip on what you were taught, whether in personal conversation or by our letter. May Jesus himself and God our Father, who reached out in love and surprised you with gifts of unending help and confidence, put a fresh heart in you, invigorate your work, enliven your speech.

—THE MESSAGE

GLOSSARY

This glossary lists key New Age terms used throughout this book. Unless otherwise indicated, definitions are from *Merriam-Webster's Collegiate Dictionary, Tenth Edition* (Merriam-Webster, Incorporated, 1995). Definitions printed in *italics* are abstracted from the text itself.

Abductees: *persons who claim to have been captured by UFO aliens for experimental purposes.*

Allopathic medicine: *a term used by New Agers to describe conventional medicine.*

Archetype: the original pattern or model of which all things of the same type are representations or copies; an inherited idea or mode of thought in the psychology of C. G. Jung that is derived from the experience of the race and is present in the unconscious of the individual.

Auditing: *a listening process in which engrams are erased from the reactive mind and stored in the analytic mind where they can be dealt with rationally.*

Bliss: *a state of enlightenment; a journey reflecting the personal development of the individual.*

Channeling: a form of mediumship in which information is communicated from a source perceived to be different from the conscious self . . . the delivery of religious or spiritual information allegedly obtained from spiritual sources, such as highly evolved and nonphysical entities (*Encyclopedia of Mystical and Paranormal Experiences*).

Collective unconscious: the genetically determined part of the unconscious that especially in the psychoanalytic theory of C. G. Jung occurs in all the members of a people or race.

Contactees: persons serving as a go-between, messenger, connection, or special source of information from a person or object in space.

Cosmic: of or relating to the cosmos, the extraterrestrial vastness, or the universe in contrast to the earth alone.

Cult: a system of religious beliefs and ritual; also: its body of adherents; a religion regarded as unorthodox or spurious.

Dianetics: the "modern science of mental health"; forerunner to Scientology (*Encyclopedia Britannica, Fifteenth Edition,* 1981).

E-meter: *electrometer; skin galvanometer used to locate engrams.*

Engrams: a hypothetical change in neural tissue postulated in order to account for persistence of memory; *disturbing memories of emotionally or physically painful experiences.*

Enlightenment: *various techniques—such as Zen meditation, biofeedback, channeling, crystals, out-of-body experiences, firewalking—used by New Agers for subjective experiences.*

Gnosticism: the thought and practice especially of various cults of late pre-Christian and early Christian centuries distinguished by the conviction that matter is evil and that emancipation comes through gnosis (esoteric knowledge).

Hero: *the self, with great creative powers which can be released, if one is willing, to achieve a state of bliss.*

Holistic health: *person oriented rather than disease oriented; treatment of the whole person—body, mind, emotion, spirit.*

Karma: the force generated by a person's actions, held in Hinduism and Buddhism to perpetuate transmigration and in its ethical consequences to determine the nature of the person's next existence.

Meditation: a discourse intended to express its author's reflections or to guide others in contemplation.

Metaphysics: abstract philosophical studies; a study of what is outside objective experience.

Monism: the belief that all that is, is one. All is interrelated, interdependent, and interpenetrating. Ultimately, there is no difference between God, a person, a carrot, or a rock. They are all part of one continuous reality that has no boundaries, no ultimate divisions (Douglas R. Groothuis, *Unmasking the New Age*).

Monomyth: *an archetype of the hero found in many societies around the world and down through history.*

Mysticism: the experience of mystical union or direct communion with ultimate reality reported by mystics; the belief that direct knowledge of God, spiritual truth, or ultimate reality can be attained through subjective experience (as intuition or insight).

Mythology: an allegorical narrative; a body of myths: as the myths dealing with the gods, demigods, and legendary heroes of a particular people.

New Age: of, relating to, or being a late twentieth century social movement drawing on ancient concepts especially from Eastern and American Indian traditions and incorporating such themes as holism, concern for nature, spirituality, and metaphysics.

Occult: matters regarded as involving the action or influence of supernatural or supernormal powers or some secret knowledge of them.

Out-of-body experience: an experience relating to or involving a feeling of separation from one's body and of being able to view oneself and others from an external perspective.

Reincarnation: rebirth in new bodies or forms of life.

Scientology: *religio-scientific movement originated in the early 1950s by L. Ron Hubbard in the United States (Encyclopedia Britannica, Fifteenth Edition, 1981).*

Synchronicity: the coincidental occurrence of events and especially psychic events (as similar thoughts in widely separated persons or a mental image of an unexpected event before it happens) that seem related but are not explained by conventional mechanisms of causality.

Taoism: a Chinese mystical philosophy . . . that teaches conformity to the Tao by unassertive action and simplicity; a religion developed from Taoist philosophy and folk and Buddhist religion and concerned with obtaining long life and good fortune often by magical means.

Theta: *the source of all life, the ground of all being.*

Thetan: *a spirit being temporarily living in the human body as an individual expression of theta.*

UFO: an unidentified flying object; especially: flying saucer.

Walk-in: *a highly developed discarnate entity who takes over the body and personality of an incarnate adult in order to raise spiritual consciousness.*

RESOURCES

The author acknowledges varying degrees of indebtedness to the following works, most of which were quoted or described in the text of this book:

Adamski, George. *Flying Saucers Farewell.* New York: Abelard-Schuman, 1961. Reprinted as *Behind the Flying Saucer Mystery,* ed. by C. A. Honey. New York: Paperback Library, 1967.

_____. *Inside the Space Ships.* New York: Abelard-Schuman, 1955. Reprinted as *Inside the Flying Saucers.* New York: Paperback Library, 1967. Revised edition, Vista, Calif.: George Adamski Foundation, 1980.

_____. *Pioneers of Space: A Trip to the Moon, Mars and Venus.* Los Angeles: Leonard-Freefield Co., 1949.

_____. *Questions and Answers by the Royal Order of Tibet: Wisdom of the Masters of the Far East,* Vol. 1. Laguna Beach: Royal Order of Tibet, 1936.

Albrecht, Mark C. *Reincarnation: A Christian Critique of a New Age Doctrine.* Downers Grove, Ill.: InterVarsity Press, 1982.

Alnor, William. *UFOs in the New Age: Extraterrestrial Messages and the Truth of Scripture.* Grand Rapids: Baker Book House, 1992.

Barker, Gray. *Gray Barker's Book of Adamski.* Clarksburg, W. Va.: Saucerian Books, 1966.

Berger, Albert. "Toward a Science of the Nuclear Mind: Science-Fiction Origins of Dianetics." *Science-Fiction Studies,* 16: 123-144, 1989.

Campbell, Joseph. *The Hero with a Thousand Faces.* New York: Pantheon, 1949.

_____. *The Masks of God: Primitive Mythology.* New York: Viking, 1959.

———. *The Masks of God: Oriental Mythology.* New York: Viking, 1962.

———. *The Masks of God: Occidental Mythology.* New York: Viking, 1964.

———. *The Masks of God: Creative Mythology.* New York: Viking, 1968.

———. *The Power of Myth.* New York: Doubleday, 1988.

Campbell, Joseph, ed. *The Portable Jung.* New York: Viking, 1971.

Campbell, Joseph, and Henry Morton Robinson. *A Skeleton Key to Finnegan's Wake.* New York: Harcourt, Brace, and World, 1944.

Campolo, Tony. *How to Rescue the Earth Without Worshipping Nature.* Milton Keynes, England: Word Publishing, 1992.

Capra, Fritjof. *The Tao of Physics: An Exploration of the Parallels Between Modern Physics and Eastern Mysticism.* Boston: Shambhala Publications, Inc., 1975.

———. *The Turning Point: Science, Society, and the Rising Culture.* New York: Simon and Schuster, 1982.

———. 1988. *Uncommon Wisdom.* New York: Bantam Books, 1988.

Capra, Fritjof, and Sharlene Spretnak. *Green Politics.* New York: Dutton, 1984.

Capra, Fritjof, and David Steindl-Rast. *Belonging to the Universe: Explorations on the Frontiers of Science and Spirituality.* New York: Harper Collins, 1991.

Chandler, Russell. *Understanding the New Age.* Dallas: Word Publishing, 1988.

Chopra, Deepak. *Ageless Body, Timeless Mind.* New York: Harmony Books, 1993.

"Chopra, Oprah? Oprah, Chopra?" *Youthworker Update,* July, 1996.

Church, Leslie F., editor, and Gerald W. Peterman, revising editor. *The NIV Matthew Henry Commentary in One Volume.* Grand Rapids: Zondervan Publishing House, A Division of Harper Collins Publishers, 1992.

Cousins, Norman. *Anatomy of an Illness as Perceived by the Patient.* New York: Norton, 1979.

———. *The Celebration of Life: A Dialogue on Hope, Spirit, and the Immortality of the Soul.* New York: Harper & Row, 1974.

———. *Dr. Schweitzer of Lambarene.* New York: Harper, 1960.

———. *Head First: The Biology of Hope and the Healing Power of the Human.* New York: Penguin Books, 1989.

———. *Human Options.* New York: W. W. Norton & Company, 1981.

———. *The Impossible Triumvirate.* New York: Norton, 1972.

———. "Modern Man Is Obsolete." *Saturday Review,* 1945.

Croydon, Bent, and L. Ron Hubbard, Jr. *L. Ron Hubbard, Messiah or Madman?* Secaucus, N.J: Lyle Stuart Inc., 1987.

D'Antonio, Michael. *Heaven on Earth.* New York: Crown Publishers, 1992.

DeVos, Peter. *Earthkeeping: Christian Stewardship of Natural Resources, Revised Edition.* Grand Rapids: Eerdmans Publishing Co., 1991.

DeWitt, Calvin. *Earth-Wise: A Biblical Response to Environmental Issues.* Grand Rapids: CRC Publications, 1994.

Dossey, Larry. *Healing Words: The Power of Prayer and the Practice of Medicine.* New York: Harper Collins, 1993.

Ferguson, Marilyn. *The Aquarian Conspiracy; Personal and Social Transformation in the 1980s.* Los Angeles: J. P. Tarcher, Inc., 1980.

Festinger, Leon. *When Prophecy Fails.* Minneapolis: University of Minnesota Press, 1956.

Frazer, Sir James. *The Golden Bough.* New York: Criterion Books, 1959.

Fuller, John G. "The Airmen Who Would Not Die." *The Reader's Digest,* June, 1979, pp. 196-246.

Fuller, Robert C. *Alternative Medicine and American Religious Life.* New York: Oxford University Press, 1989.

Gardner, Martin. *The New Age: Notes of a Fringe Watcher.* Buffalo, N.Y.: Prometheus, 1988.

Geisler, Norman. *Religion of the Force.* Dallas: Quest, 1983.

Golden, Kenneth L., editor. *Uses of Comparative Mythology: Essays on the Work of Joseph Campbell.* New York: Garland Publishing, Inc., 1992.

Goleman, Daniel, and Joel Gurin, editors. *Mind Body Medicine: How to Use Your Mind for Better Health.* Yonkers, New York: Consumer Reports Books, 1993.

Gordon, Henry. *Channeling into the New Age: the "Teachings" of Shirley MacLaine and Other Such Gurus: an Unauthorized Account.* Buffalo, N.Y.: Prometheus, 1988.

Graham, Billy. *Angels: God's Secret Agents,* Revised and Expanded Edition. Waco: Word Books, 1986.

Gray, William. *Thinking Critically About New Age Ideas.* Belmont, Calif.: Wadsworth Publishing Co., 1991.

Groothuis, Douglas. *Confronting the New Age: How to Resist a Growing Religious Movement.* Downers Grove, Ill.: InterVarsity Press, 1988.

_____. *Revealing the New Age Jesus.* Downers Grove, Ill.: InterVarsity Press, 1990.

_____. *Unmasking the New Age.* Downers Grove, Ill.: InterVarsity Press, 1986.

Guiley, Rosemary Ellen. *Harper's Encyclopedia of Mystical & Paranormal Experience.* New York: Harper Collins, 1991.

The Heidelberg Catechism. Grand Rapids: CRC Publications, 1975, 1988.

Heinlein, Robert. *Stranger in a Strange Land.* New York: G. P. Putnam's Sons, 1961.

Herbert, Nick. *Quantum Reality: Beyond the New Physics.* Garden City, New York: Anchor Press, 1985.

Hopkins, Budd. *Intruders.* New York: Ballantine, 1992.

Hoyt, Karen, and J. Isamu Yamamoto. *The New Age Rage.* New York: Flemming H. Revell, 1987.

Hubbard, L. Ron. *Dianetics: The Modern Science of Mental Health,* Second Edition. Los Angeles: Bridge Publications, 1985.

_____. *Scientology.* Los Angeles: Bridge Publications, 1988.

Hunt, Dave, and T.A. McMahon. *America: The Sorcerer's New Apprentice.* Eugene, Oregon: Harvest House Publishers, 1988.

Hynek, J. Allen. *The UFO Experience: A Scientific Inquiry.* Chicago: H. Regnery Co., 1972.

Jones, Peter. *The Gnostic Empire Strikes Back: An Old Heresy for the New Age.* Phillipsburg, N.J.: Presbyterian and Reformed Publishing Company, 1992.

Jung, Carl. *Flying Saucers: A Modern Myth of Things Seen in the Sky.* New York: New American Library, 1959.

Larsen, Stephen, and Robin Larsen. *A Fire in the Mind.* New York: Doubleday, 1991.

Leslie, Desmond, and George Adamski. *Flying Saucers Have Landed.* New York: British Books, 1953. Revised Edition, 1970.

Lewis, C. S. *Mere Christianity.* New York: Macmillan, 1952.

Lewis, James, ed. *The Gods Have Landed: New Religions from Other Worlds.* Albany, New York: State University of New York Press, 1995.

Lewis, James R., and J. Gordon Melton. *Perspectives on the New Age.* Albany, New York: State University of New York Press, 1992.

Lovelock, James E. "Gaia: the World as Living Organism." *New Scientist,* 1986, pp. 25-8.

Lutzer, Erwin, and John F. DeVries. *Satan's "Evangelistic" Strategy for This New Age.* Wheaton: Victor Books, 1989.

MacLaine, Shirley. *Dancing in the Light.* New York: Bantam Books, 1985.

_____. *Don't Fall Off the Mountain.* New York: Norton, 1970.

_____. *It's All in the Playing.* New York: Bantam, 1987.

_____. *Out on a Limb.* New York: Bantam Books, 1983.

_____. *You Can't Get There from Here.* New York: Bantam Books, 1975.

McGuire, Meredith B. *Ritual Healing in Suburban America.* New Brunswick, N.J.: Rutgers University Press, 1988.

Melton, J. Gordon. *New Age Almanac.* New York: Visible Ink, 1991.

_____. *Encyclopedia of American Religions, Fourth Edition.* Detroit: Gale Research Co., 1993.

Merriam-Webster's Collegiate Dictionary, Tenth Edition. Springfield, MA: Merriam-Webster, Inc., 1987.

Miller, Elliot. *A Crash Course on the New Age Movement: Describing and Evaluating a Growing Social Force.* Grand Rapids: Baker Book House, 1989.

Miller, Russell. *Bare-Faced Messiah: The True Story of L. Ron Hubbard.* New York: Henry Holt and Company, 1987.

Montgomery, Ruth. *Strangers Among Us.* New York: Coward, 1979.

Morris, Richard. *Dismantling the Universe: the Nature of Scientific Discovery.* New York: Simon and Schuster, 1983.

Morth, Ingo. "Elements of Religious Meaning in Science-Fiction Literature." *Social Compass,* 1986, pp. 87-108.

The NIV Study Bible, New International Version. Grand Rapids: Zondervan Corporation, 1985.

Norman, Ruth. *Tesla Speaks.* El Cajon, Calif.: Unarius-Science of Life, 1974.

Our World Belongs to God, A Contemporary Testimony, Study Edition. Grand Rapids: CRC Publications, 1987.

Pagels, Elaine. *The Gnostic Gospels.* New York: Random House, 1979.

Persinger, Michael A., and J. S. Derr. "Geophysical Variables and Behavior; Temporal Coupling of UFO Reports and Seismic Energy Release Within the Rio Grande Rift System: Discriminative Validity of the Techtonic Strain Theory." *Perceptual and Motor Skills,* October, 1990, pp. 531-6.

Peters, Ted. *The Cosmic Self.* San Francisco: Harper SanFrancisco, 1991.

Randles, Jenny, and Peter Warrington. *Science and the UFOs.* Cambridge: Basil Blackwell, 1985.

Reisser, Paul C. *New Age Medicine.* Downers Grove, Ill.: InterVarsity Press, 1987.

Rhodes, Ron. *The Counterfeit Christ of the New Age Movement.* Grand Rapids: Baker Book House, 1990.

_____. *New Age Movement.* Grand Rapids: Zondervan Publishing House, 1995.

Rich, Adrienne. *Of Women Born.* New York: Norton, 1976.

Robinson, Henry Morton. *The Cardinal.* New York: Simon and Schuster, 1950.

Schucman, Helen Cohen. *A Course in Miracles.* Farmington, N.Y.: Foundation for Inner Peace, 1981.

Schweitzer, Albert. *Out of My Life and Thought: an Autobiography.* New York: Holt, 1949.

Segal, Robert. *Joseph Campbell, An Introduction.* New York: Mentor.

Siegel, Bernie. *Love, Medicine, and Miracles.* New York: Harper Collins, 1990.

Sire, James. *Shirley MacLaine and the New Age Movement.* Downers Grove, Ill.: InterVarsity Press, 1988.

_____. *The Universe Next Door.* Downers Grove, Ill.: InterVarsity Press, 1988.

Smith, F. LaGard. *Out On a Broken Limb.* Eugene, Oreg.: Harvest House Publishers, 1986.

Snyder, John. *Reincarnation vs. Resurrection.* Chicago: Moody Press, 1984.

Strieber, Whitley. *Communion.* New York: Avon Books, 1987.

Stupple, David. "The Man Who Talked with Venusians." *Fate,* January, 1979, p. 39.

_____. "Mahatmas and Space Brothers: the Ideologies of Alleged Contact with Extraterrestrials." *Journal of American Culture,* Spring/Summer, 1984, pp. 131-139.

Tipton, Steven M. *Getting Saved from the Sixties.* Berkeley: University of California Press, 1982.

Vallee, Jacques. *Messengers of Deception.* Berkley: And/Or Press, 1979.

_____. *Confrontations: A Scientist's Search for Alien Contact.* New York: Ballantine Books, 1990.

Von Daniken, Erich. *Chariots of the Gods?: Unsolved Mysteries of the Past.* New York: G. P. Putnam's Sons, 1968.

Wallis, Claudia. "Faith and Healing." *Time,* June 24, 1996, pp. 59-68.

Whitehead, Harriet. *Renunciation and Reformulation: A Study of Conversion in an American Sect.* Ithica, N.Y.: Cornell University Press, 1987.

Williamson, Marianne. *A Return to Love.* New York; Harper Collins, 1992.

Winbish, David. *Something's Going On Out There.* Old Tappan, N.Y.: Revell, 1990.

Yancey, Phillip. *The Jesus I Never Knew.* Grand Rapids: Zondervan Publishing House, 1995.

York, Michael. *The Emerging Network: A Sociology of the New Age and Neo-pagan Movement.* Lanham, Md.: Rowman & Littlefield Publishers, Inc., 1995.

Zinsstag, Lou and Timothy Good. *George Adamski—The Untold Story.* Beckenham, Ky.: Ceti Publications, 1983.

Zukav, Gary. *The Dancing Wu Li Masters: An Overview of the New Physics.* New York: William Morrow and Company, Inc., 1979.

Other books in the series include:
- *TRADING PLACES: Caring for Elderly Parents*
- *NEW BEGINNINGS: Divorce and Remarriage in the Christian Community*
- *WHAT REALLY MATTERS: Passing on Your Family Values*
- *EARTH-WISE: A Biblical Response to Environmental Issues*
- *TOO CLOSE FOR COMFORT: Understanding and Responding to the Reality of Abuse*
- *THE BOTTOM LINE: Making Christian Choices in the Marketplace*
- *A FAMILY AFFAIR: Worshipping God with Our Children*
- *DAD'S DYING: A Family's Journey Through Death*
- *WHO'S IN CHARGE? A Biblical Approach to Parenting*
- *CALL ME WHEN YOU'RE 20! A Parent's Guide to Living with Teens*